W9-CNP-121

COUNTERPARTS

AN INTERMEDIATE READING PROGRAM

Second Edition

By Beverly Pimsleur

with Linda Lee

Heinle & Heinle Publishers
A division of International Thomson Publishing, Inc.
Boston, Massachusetts 02116 U.S.A.
The ITP logo is a trademark under license.

Pacific Grove • Albany • Bonn • Boston • Cincinnati • Detroit • London • Madrid • Melbourne
Mexico City • New York • Paris • San Francisco • Tokyo • Toronto • Washington

The publication of *Counterparts, Second Edition,* was directed by the members of the Newbury House Publishing Team at Heinle & Heinle:

Erik Gundersen, Editorial Director
John F. McHugh, Market Development Director
Kristin Thalheimer, Production Services Coordinator

Also participating in the publication of this program were:

Publisher: Stanley J. Galek
Editorial Production Manager: Elizabeth Holthaus
Project Manager: Judy Keith
Assistant Editor: Karen P. Hazar
Production Assistant: Maryellen Eschmann
Manufacturing Coordinator: Mary Beth Hennebury
Photo Researcher: Denise Theodores
Page Layout: Christine E. Wilson, IBC
Interior Designer: Julia Getcha
Illustrator: Bob Doucet
Cover Artist: Erik Gundersen

Library of Congress Cataloging-in-Publication Data

Pimsleur, Beverly
    Counterparts, an intermediate reader / by Beverly Pimsleur with
Linda Lee. —2nd. ed.
        p.   cm.
    ISBN 0-8384-5006-7
    1. English language—Textbooks for foreign speakers. 2. United
States—Civilization—Problems, exercises, etc. 3. Readers—United
States. I. Lee, Linda, 1950- . II. Title.
PE1128.P52 1995
428.6'4—dc20
                94-22498
                CIP

Copyright © 1995 by Heinle & Heinle Publishers
All rights reserved. No part of this publication may be reproduced or transmitted in any form or by any means, electronic or mechanical, including photocopy, recording, or any information storage and retrieval system, without permission in writing from the publisher.

Heinle & Heinle Publishers / A Division of International Thomson Publishing, Inc.

Manufactured in the United States of America
ISBN 0-8384-5006-7

10 9 8 7

This new edition of COUNTERPARTS has been completly revised to reflect some new topical concerns in American life and to incorporate innovative pedagogical developments in the teaching of reading. This edition includes pre-reading questions and a thoroughly expanded exercise program. The diverse selection of stories, as in the First Edition, reflects topics that are of current concern in North American life.

COUNTERPARTS was written for English-as-a-Second or Foreign Language students who wish to improve their reading and communication skills for a variety of academic, personal, or professional reasons. In addition, COUNTERPARTS can be adapted for use by native speakers in developmental reading classes and has also been used effectively by high school students.

The new chapters added to the Second Edition cover a variety of provocative topics. *Daisy Chin-Lor* recounts the difficult choices of a young woman balancing her cultural heritage and family with a career commitment. *Body Language Speaks Louder Than Words* proposes that men and women "speak a different body language" reflecting their functions in social and business situations. Other new chapters treat the following subjects: *Citizenship: A Difficult Choice, Elderhostel: Active Life after 60,* and *Protecting the Environment.* A number of readings from the previous edition have been updated where necessary.

As in the First Edition, the chapter topics were selected for their inherent interest, for what they reflect of current North American society, their appeal to a variety of readers varying in age and background, and their ability to stimulate meaningful classroom discussions. The exercises at the end of each chapter include a wide variety of activities, some new to this edition. Pre-reading questions have been added to help students relate the chapter topics to their own experiences and to make predictions about the content of the reading passages. The **Vocabulary in Context** and the **Counterparts** sections have been revised and expanded. A new section, **Comprehension and Discussion,** gives the students the opportunity to further explore their ideas about the theme of the readings. This section provides rich and stimulating material for classroom exchanges, using the diversity of cultural backgrounds of the students.

There is no attempt to make this a definitive book about North American culture, but by the time the students have finished it, they will be better acquainted with the diversity of life in the United States and Canada. They will also have expanded their use of vocabulary in a variety of subjects and had ample opportunity to improve their skills in the integrated disciplines of reading, speaking, and writing.

The reading selections for COUNTERPARTS were taken primarily from contemporary newspapers and magazines. Books and television commentaries were used where the subject matter and vocabulary were thought to be of particular interest and value for teaching. An attempt was made to increase the level of difficulty in subject matter, vocabulary, and sentence structure from the beginning of the book to the end. In general, the book moves toward more difficult subjects at the end when students have an improved facility with the language and are better prepared to have in-depth discussions.

The photographs are intended to be an important and integral part of COUNTERPARTS. They illustrate various aspects of the readings and, in some cases, offer different points of view from the ones expressed in the articles. Teachers are encouraged to use the photographs as creatively and often as possible. They provide wonderful prompts for activating background knowledge and effective tools for engaging students in the activities that follow each reading.

An Answer Key to all of the exercises and activities in COUNTERPARTS, Second Edition, is available separately from Heinle & Heinle Publishers.

B. P.

CONTENTS

ACKNOWLEDGMENTS

"Daisy Chin-Lor," excerpt from *Rosy Grier's All-American Heroes* by Roosevelt Grier. Copyright © 1993 MasterMedia. Reprinted by permission of MasterMedia Limited, New York (800) 334-8232.

"Underwater Concerts," adapted from *New Music Makes a Big Splash at UCSD Pool* by Michael Granberry in the Los Angeles Times, 7 April 1982. Copyright © 1982 LA Times. Reprinted by permission of the Los Angeles Times.

"Citizenship," from *Immigrants Forgoing Citizenship While Pursuing American Dream* by Deborah Sontag, July 25, 1993. *Civics Lesson/The Route to Citizenship*, accompanying graphic by Megan Jaegerman, July 25, 1993. *Immigration/Leaving the Green Card Behind*, accompanying graph, July 25, 1993. Copyright © 1993 by The New York Times Company. Reprinted by permission.

About Men: Conflicting Interests by Donald H. Bell, July 31, 1983. Copyright © 1983 by The New York Times Company. Reprinted by permission.

"An Alternative: Mothers Who Return Home," from *Mothers Who Shift Back from Jobs to Homemaking* by Judy Klemesrud, January 19, 1983. Copyright © 1983 by The New York Times Company. Reprinted by permission.

"Elderhostel: Active Life After Age 60," article from the Public Relations Department of Elderhostel, Boston, MA. Reprinted by permission.

"Alone Versus Lonely," from *Personal Health: Alone v Lonely* by Jane E. Brody, April 6, 1983. Copyright © 1983 by The New York Times Company. Reprinted by permission.

"It's the Real Thing: People as Art," adapted from *Duane Hanson* by Roy Bongartz in Horizon magazine, September 1977. Reprinted by permission of the author.

"Uses for the Zodiac: Love and License Plates," adapted from *Love and Astrology* by Sybil Leek (New York: Berkley, 1981). Copyright © 1981 by Sybil Leek. Reprinted by permission of Lou Reda Productions; and from a CBC broadcast of "Ontario This Week," 19 March 1983, interview by Judy Darling.

"The Chili Cookoff: Some Like it Hot," adapted from an *Out Yonder* column by Ross McSwain in the San Angelo Standard Times, 2 November, 1981. Reprinted by permission of the author.

"Body Language Speaks Louder Than Words" by Janet Lee Mills, Associate Dean, College of Social Sciences & Public Affairs, Boise State University. Reprinted by permission of the author.

"The Story of Shin's Family Store," adapted from *Making It* by Michael Daly in the New York Magazine, 20 December 1982. Reprinted by permission of the author.

"Protecting the Environment" from *Living in the Environment, 7/e* by G. Tyler Miller Jr. Copyright © 1992 Wadsworth Publishing Co. Reprinted by permission of Wadsworth Publishing Co., Ca.

Excerpt from *Honoring Vietnam Veterans-At Last* by Morganthau. From NEWSWEEK 11/22/82. Copyright © 1982, Newsweek, Inc. All rights reserved. Reprinted by permission. Excerpt from *Remembering a War We Want to Forget* by William Broyles. From NEWSWEEK 11/22/82. Copyright © 1982, Newsweek, Inc. All rights reserved. Reprinted by permission. *Vietnam Memorial: Touching, Tears, Roses, Rain,"* by Phil Gailey, August 30, 1983 (excerpt). Copyright © 1983 by The New York Times Company. Reprinted by permission. *What Happens When a Woman Designs a War Monument* by Michael Sorkin in Vogue, May 1983. Copyright © 1983 by The Condé Nast Publications, Inc. Reprinted courtesy of Vogue. *Vietnam War Memorial* in ARTnews, January 1983. Copyright © January 1983. Reprinted with the permission of ARTnews. Excerpt (adapted) from *What's in a Name?* in The New Republic, 6 December 1982. Copyright © 1982 The New Republic, Inc. Reprinted by permission of The New Republic.

2, 5, 9 Courtesy of Daisy Chin-Lor; 12 Gerard Mondenx-Vian/Sygma; 14 Philippe Bastin; 15 C. J. Perrin; 22 Jim Estrin/NYT Pictures; 32 Elizabeth Crews/Stock, Boston; 35 Joan Tedeschi/Comstock; 42 Elizabeth Crews/The Image Works; 45 Elizabeth Crews/Stock Boston; 52, 55 Jim Harrison; 64 Michael Dwyer/Stock Boston; 73 Courtesy of Helander Gallery. Photo: Michael Price; 75, 76, 77 Courtesy of Helander Gallery; 91 Department Library Services, American Museum of Natural History; 92 Laila Zuejnieks/Ministry of Transportation, Toronto; 100 Jo Ann Horton; 102, 103 Bob Daemmrich Photography; 112-115 Janet Lee Mills; 123 Courtesy of the Isamu Noguchi Foundation, Inc., Photo by Vytas Valaitis; 124 Courtesy of the Isamu Noguchi Foundation, Inc., Photo by Shigeo Anzai; 126 Courtesy of the Isamu Noguchi Foundation, Inc., Photo by Isamu Noguchi; 134, 137, 141 Harry Benson; 149 Greenpeace/Morgan; 151 David J. Cross; 158 Joyce R. Wilson/Photo Researchers Inc.; 163 Janice Rogovin/The Picture Cube; 164 Three Servicemen Statue ©1984. F.E. Hart/VVMF. Vietnam Veterans Memorial, Washington, D.C., Photo: Jim Burns; 165 ©Vietnam Women's Memorial Project, Inc., Glenna Goodacre, sculptor. Photo: Gregory Staley

COUNTERPARTS

Daisy Chin-Lor: A Successful Businesswoman

1. Have you ever worked in business? What was your experience?

2. What skills and personal qualities does a person need to become a successful business executive? What special problems might women executives face?

3. Study the photographs in this chapter. Based on the photographs, what do you know about Daisy Chin-Lor, the business executive in this article?

CHAPTER 1

From the time she was a child, Daisy Chin-Lor understood that she was expected to work hard, to set an example, to make something of herself. She had her family's unflagging° support in whatever choice she made, in whatever she did, as long as she was trying to be the best person she could possibly be. For her family, the desire to excel° was treated almost as a credo°—push yourself and your dreams will come true.

> constant
>
> do things very well
> belief

Chin-Lor's parents were even willing to leave their homeland, China, to fulfill their dreams. They came to America in 1945, arriving in postwar New York in
search of a better life for themselves, and most importantly, their children.

They were determined to live the American dream. And as they raised their family, they instilled in° Chin-Lor and her sisters a belief that anything was possible if they believed in themselves and their own potential.°

> **instilled in:** put an idea in someone's mind
>
> capacity for growth or development
>
> be the first to try

The children were also taught that they had a responsibility to set a positive example, to pioneer° a "different path" for Asians in the United States, Chin-Lor recalled.

"I grew up in a predominantly white neighborhood, and our family represented Asians to our neighbors as well as what others might think of *all* Asians. Because of that, my parents instilled in my sisters and me the 'mission'° to stand out among the crowd, to be the best and set an example for all Asians. Being really different created in me an urge° to excel, to walk ahead and not look back, and to set an example for future generations."

> duty
>
> strong desire

Chin-Lor has more than succeeded at that mission. Today, she is a highly successful and respected business executive who has worked around the globe for one of the world's largest corporations, and she is widely regarded as a leader in the Asian-American community.

Chin-Lor has been married for fifteen years to Rolland Lor, an entrepreneur who has his own trading company based in New York and Hong Kong. They have one son, eleven-year-old Jonathan.

Like most working women, Chin-Lor sometimes faces

difficult/does several things at a time

personal opinions or conclusions

things that need attention first

Phi Beta Kappa: an organization of university students whose members are chosen because of their high academic standing

retail chain: a group of stores under one ownership

prestige fragrances: expensive perfumes

involving possible loss/quick advancement

advancement in one's job or career

tough° choices as she juggles° the complex demands of a family and a successful business career. But she wouldn't have it any other way.

"For me, success is being able to balance my career, my family life, and my personal interests, and getting the most fulfillment and enjoyment possible out of each," she said.

Asked how she achieves that balance, Chin-Lor offered these insights:°

"Find the right people and systems that will support your demanding lifestyle. Focus on time management, set clear priorities,° and be realistic about what can be done.

"Don't be afraid to say 'no,' or ask for help. And be proud of making the choice to have both a career and a family."

Chin-Lor began her business career not long after graduating Phi Beta Kappa° in 1975 from Hunter College in New York. Her first job was as a buyer for Sears & Roebuck Company, which, at the time, was the nation's largest retail chain.° She worked for Sears for five years, until the company relocated to Chicago.

Chin-Lor wanted to stay in New York to be close to her parents and two sisters, so she began a job search that led her to Avon Products, Inc., the world's largest direct marketer of beauty and related products. She joined the company in 1979 as a product counselor in its New York-based jewelry marketing group.

As she has done throughout her life, Chin-Lor excelled at Avon. She quickly rose through the company's marketing ranks, being named group marketing manager for prestige fragrances° within five years.

Chin-Lor then took what many people might have considered a risky° career move—she left the fast-track° marketing group to join human resources as Avon's director of multicultural planning. The move paid off by giving Chin-Lor broader business experience. Within two years, Avon offered her a major promotion:° an international position as the company's area director in Europe.

That promotion presented a turning point in her life and a test of her desire to balance work and family. "Clearly, it was the right career move," Chin-Lor said, "but it also was a major sacrifice for my husband, who had to give up his job; for my son, who had to relocate and make new friends; and for my parents, who were going to miss me."

Ever supportive of her success, Chin-Lor's family willingly made the sacrifices required for her to accept the promotion abroad. The move was a good one: after two years in Europe, Chin-Lor was sent to Hong Kong as a regional director for Avon's Pacific markets. Then, in 1991, she was promoted again, this time to a highly visible post in a very competitive market—the kind of job that's coveted° in most multinational corporations.

very desirable

At the relatively young age of 38, Chin-Lor became president of Avon's subsidiary° in Taiwan, one of the company's fastest-growing and most profitable° businesses. As president of Avon Cosmetics Taiwan, Ltd., Chin-Lor runs a multimillion-dollar company with three hundred full-time employees and a sales force of forty thousand. She currently is one of only two women presidents among Avon's thirty-eight subsidiaries worldwide.

a company with more than half of its stock owned by another company

earning more money than it spends

For Chin-Lor, being named president of a key Avon business wasn't just a tribute° to her own hard work and determination, it was a tribute to the love and support her parents and family had given for years.

acknowledgement

EXERCISES

I.   Comprehension and Discussion Questions

General Ideas
1.   In Chin-Lor's family, what personal qualities are valued?
2.   What career choices did Chin-Lor make? How did these choices affect her career and family?
3.   What problems has she faced?
4.   How does she define success?

Details
5.   Scan the reading to find answers to these questions:
   a.   Why did Chin-Lor's parents move to the United States?
   b.   How many children does Chin-Lor have?
   c.   What was her first job?
   d.   What job does she have now?

Opinions
6.   How would you describe Chin-Lor?
7.   In what ways is Chin-Lor a successful person?
8.   Would you like to follow a similar career path? Why or why not?

II.   Sequencing Exercise

Number the events in Chin-Lor's life in the order in which they occurred.

_____   She became the area director for Avon's products in Europe.

_____   Avon Products, Inc., offered her a job as a product counselor.

_____   She graduated from Hunter College in New York.

_____   She became president of Avon's subsidiary in Taiwan.

_____   She got a job with the largest retail chain in the United States.

_____   She moved to Hong Kong, where she worked as the regional director for Avon Products, Inc.

_____   She left marketing and took a position in Avon's human resources division.

_____   She was promoted to group marketing manager for prestige fragrances.

III. Vocabulary in Context

Use context—the words and ideas around an unfamiliar word—to guess the meaning of the italicized words below. Then look up each word in a dictionary. Choose the dictionary definition that best fits the meaning of the word in this context.

1. "I grew up in a *predominantly* white neighborhood, and our family represented Asians to our neighbors as well as what others might think of <u>all</u> Asians."

   My guess: _____

   Dictionary definition: _____

2. Today, Chin-Lor is a highly successful and respected business executive who has worked around the *globe* for one of the world's largest corporations.

   My guess: _____

   Dictionary definition: _____

3. Chin-Lor has been married for fifteen years to Rolland Lor, an *entrepreneur* who has his own trading company based in New York.

   My guess: _____

   Dictionary definition: _____

4. Chin-Lor worked for Sears for five years, until the company *relocated* to Chicago. She wanted to stay in New York to be close to her parents and two sisters, so she began a job search that led her to Avon Products, Inc.

   My guess: _____

   Dictionary definition: _____

5. "Clearly it was the right career move," Chin-Lor said, "but it also was a major *sacrifice* for my husband, who had to give up his job; for my son, who had to relocate and make new friends; and for my parents, who were going to miss me."

   My guess: _____

   Dictionary definition: _____

6. In 1991, Chin-Lor was promoted again, this time to a highly visible *post* in a very competitive market—the kind of job that's coveted in most multinational corporations.

   My guess: _____

   Dictionary definition: _____

IV.　Word Forms

Put the correct form of the word in each blank. Check the verb forms for tense, number, and voice (active or passive), and check the nouns for number (singular or plural).

1.　determination (n)　determine (v)　determined (adj)

　　a.　She doesn't lack _____; when she decides to do something, she does it.

　　b.　Although he has never worked in a restaurant, he is _____ to own one someday.

　　c.　You have to _____ what the problem is before you can fix it.

2.　pioneer (n)　pioneer (v)

　　a.　The first people to live in this area were called _____.

　　b.　Nicolas Cugnot _____ the horseless carriage. The modern automobile developed from this steam-powered cart.

3.　success (n)　succeed (v)　successful (adj)　successfully (adv)

　　a.　Abraham Lincoln wanted to become president of the United States and he _____. In 1861, he became the sixteenth president.

　　b.　The first steam-powered vehicle was not a _____ because the driver had to stop every 15 minutes to add water.

　　c.　Although she was having engine trouble, the pilot landed the airplane _____.

　　d.　According to Chin-Lor, if you want to be _____, you must find a way to balance the different parts of your life.

4.　support (n)　support (v)　supportive (adj)

　　a.　Not everyone _____ his decision to relocate the company to New York. Some employees want the company to stay in Chicago.

　　b.　Her parents were _____ when she decided to change jobs.

　　c.　I couldn't have made this decision without the _____ of my family.

5.　risk (n)　risk (v)　risky (adj)

　　a.　She _____ her life when she ran into the burning house to save her child.

　　b.　Before you make a decision, think about the _____.

　　c.　Starting your own business is _____ because you might lose all your money.

6.　promotion (n)　promote (v)

　　a.　When he was _____ to president of the company, he had to relocate to New York.

　　b.　If you want a _____, you will have to take some courses in accounting.

V. Sentence Completion

Complete each sentence, using one of the words listed below.

      priorities   excel   recall   highly   tough   risks   willingly   profitable

1. Thomas Edison was a(n) _____ creative person. He invented 1,093 different things.

2. If you want to _____ in your studies, you will have to work hard.

3. Finding a job is one of my _____. After I find a job, I'll look for a place to live.

4. My friend _____ took a job in California because she likes the climate there.

5. I can't _____ what she said. Do you remember?

6. It was a(n) _____ exam. I hope I passed.

7. For the first five years, his company was not _____, but after that he began to earn a lot of money.

8. You shouldn't start your own business if you don't like to take _____.

COUNTERPARTS

1. In the article, Chin-Lor defines success in this way:

    "For me, success is being able to balance my career, my family life, and my personal interests, and getting the most fulfillment and enjoyment possible out of each."

    What do you think of her definition? What is your definition of success?

2. In groups, decide if you agree or disagree with the statements below.

    a. No one can really balance career and work. If a woman chooses to be a business executive, her family will suffer. Agree or disagree? Why?

    b. Chin-Lor's ethnic background and gender helped her advance in her career. Agree or disagree? Why?

3. In this article, Chin-Lor identifies some of the values and beliefs that she learned from her parents. Take several minutes to list some of the values and beliefs that you learned from your parents. Then identify the values and beliefs that you would pass on to your children. Tell why you think these values are important.

Values and beliefs learned from parents.	Would you pass these values and beliefs to your children?		Why?
	YES	NO	
Always be honest.	✔		*When you are honest, other people respect you.*

4. Choose a career that interests you. List the skills and personal qualities that a person needs in order to succeed in this career. Read your list to the class and see if they can guess the career.

Underwater Concerts: They Float

1. Where can you go to listen to music in your area? Which is the best place?

2. What do the pictures in this chapter tell you about underwater concerts? List at least five things.

3. Michel Redolfi organizes underwater concerts. If you were a newspaper reporter, what questions would you ask him? List your questions. Then read the article to look for answers to your questions.

hey closed their eyes and began floating in the pool. The 92-degree water felt warm, giving them the illusion° of weightlessness. The music, synthesized° sounds of flutes and harps° combined with natural sounds of the deep of the ocean, enveloped the audience. Some compared the experience to life in the womb,° others to a trance;° still others said it seemed like a futuristic encounter in outer space.

"I held my breath much longer than I thought possible. The music was so beautiful. I didn't want to breathe much. But, then, I remembered that I had to, so I'd surface." These remarks were heard at one of Michel Redolfi's underwater concerts, concerts that he has organized in swimming pools and oceans all over the United States, Europe, and Canada. Redolfi, born in Marseilles, France, and currently living in San Diego, is a composer who is revolutionizing the concept of concert listening. Redolfi believes that avant-garde° music needs an equally avant-garde environment. He finds the ocean and the swimming pool natural settings for these new sounds, and his music is composed to be heard under water.

Redolfi's interest in messages from the ocean floor comes from his growing up by the Mediterranean.

The concept of underwater sounds is part of the folklore of people who live by the sea. There are stories of songs of sirens,° bells of submerged° churches, the voices of lost sailors. These tales have unfortunately been replaced in the twentieth century by the idea that the ocean is a quiet place, disturbed only by the song of the whale. The fact is the sea is full of noises, complete with fish "barking," shrimp "snapping" and dolphins° "whistling."

Redolfi first experimented with bringing these natural sounds up from the ocean depths, using special underwater microphones.° Inspired by his vision of the underwater world, he combined these sounds with computer-generated° sounds. His next, more radical step, was to bring the music into the

---

impression
electronically created
flutes and harps: (musical instruments)
place where unborn child lives/ dreamlike state

new, experimental

imaginary sea women/underwater

shrimp . . . and dolphins: (sea animals)

instruments, used in recording
created by computer

water—and the listening public with it. "Music is usually presented in concert halls," he says, "where you wear uncomfortable clothing and where you have either the best seats in the house or the worst ones." Redolfi's concerts require no more clothing than a bathing suit and an optional° mask° and snorkel.°

not required/face covering
breathing tube
of the senses

"I wanted to compose for a total sensory° experience. I wanted you to *feel* the music as well as hear it. When you are listening underwater, you can't tell where the sound is coming from. It resonates° and seems to come from within your own body. For the first time people can listen in zero gravity, like in outer space. They can move freely in any direction while listening, even upside down. Some like to drift, others dive° and frolic."°

fills with sound

go under water
play happily

Often concertgoers stay underwater, letting the music surround them and surfacing only to breathe. Others prefer to float on their backs with only their ears submerged so that they will have an uninterrupted musical experience.

The music itself is transmitted through the water by underwater speakers attached to a large, floating plastic "jellyfish." Redolfi explained, "You can hear the music only when your head is in direct contact with the water. . . . The sound waves pass through your skin as if the flesh didn't exist." Because our bodies are 80 percent water, the sound bypasses your eardrums and gets right into your skull bones, where the nerves are. From outside the pool, all you experience is a vague° electronic murmur.° Redolfi claims that if you put only your forehead in

not clear

low, soft sound

the water, you can still pick up° the music. Because of this phenomenon, Redolfi has found out that his music can be perceived by deaf people whose hearing impairment° is limited to problems with the external ear. But, Redolfi says, not enough research has been done to reach any final conclusions.

pick up: hear

limitation

In the meantime, he is pursuing his own projects, which include an idea for a pool designed only for underwater concerts, a sort of underwater opera house. "I want to broaden my sense of communication, not so much with the creatures of the ocean," he said, "but with my fellow human beings. Some of my colleagues think that I am some kind of California nut and haven't as yet showed up for any of my concerts."

But the public seems to think differently: "I feel that it is

trick/special art event
clearness/fresh, clean

definitely a new art form," said one bathing-suit-clad partici-pant, "not just a gimmick° or a happening.° I was surprised at the clarity° of the sound and its crisp° quality, I certainly think it is a great alternative to going to a movie or dinner, and it's a wonderful thing to experience with someone." Said another, "I loved it, I would even pay to hear it in a traditional concert hall." But that might not be necessary, because at the moment, there are more swimming pools in America than concert halls.

UPDATE: Mr. Redolfi has recently been appointed as Director of CIRM (International Center for Music and Research) in Nice, France where he continues his activities as composer, re-searcher, and producer of innovative music concerts.

EXERCISES

I.   Comprehension and Discussion Questions

General Ideas

1.   What is unusual about Michel Redolfi's concerts?

2.   In your own words, describe what happens at Redolfi's underwater concerts.

3.   Why is Redolfi interested in underwater concerts? What is his purpose for organizing these concerts?

Details

4.   Scan the reading to find answers to these questions:

   a.   What kind of music does Redolfi compose?

   b.   Where did he grow up?

   c.   What do people wear to Redolfi's concerts?

   d.   How is the music transmitted underwater?

   e.   What future plans does Redolfi have?

Opinions

5.   Would you like to attend an underwater concert? Why or why not?

6.   Do you think underwater concerts are a gimmick or a new art form? Why?

II.   Vocabulary in Context

Use context to choose the word or term that best fits the meaning of the italicized words in the sentences below. Circle your answers.

1. "I held my breath much longer than I thought possible. The music was so beautiful. I didn't want to breathe much. But, then, I remembered that I had to, so I'd *surface.*"

    a. stay underwater   b. turn around in the water   c. go to the top of the water

2. Redolfi believes that avant-garde music needs an equally avant-garde *environment.* He finds the ocean and the swimming pool natural settings for these new sounds.

    a. sound   b. setting   c. composer

3. Redolfi first experimented with bringing natural sounds up from the ocean depths, using special underwater microphones. His next, more *radical* step, was to bring the music into the water—and the listening public with it.

    a. unusual   b. ordinary   c. unpleasant

4. Often concertgoers stay underwater, letting the music surround them and surfacing only to breathe. Others prefer to float on their backs with only their ears *submerged* so that they will have an uninterrupted musical experience.

    a. out of the water   b. underwater   c. protected

5. The music is *transmitted* through the water by underwater speakers attached to a large, floating plastic jellyfish.

    a. heard   b. felt   c. sent

III.   Word Forms

Put the correct form of the word in each blank. Check the verb forms for correct tense, number, and voice (active or passive), and check the nouns for number (singular or plural).

1. impairment (n)   impair (v)   impaired (adj)

    a. Because of his physical _____, he could not climb steps.

    b. He enrolled his hearing _____ child in a special class.

    c. The accident permanently _____ his vision.

2. concept (n)   conception (n)   conceptual (adj)

    a. New _____ are often not immediately accepted.

    b. The lecturer began by explaining the _____ basis of her paper.

    c. My _____ of the project is very different from yours.

3. clarity (n)   clarification (n)   clarify (v)

   a. Parts of your essay require further _____.

   b. At the press conference yesterday, the senator was asked to _____ some of his previous statements.

   c. The _____ of her paintings is very striking; they seem like photographs.

4. inspire (v)   inspired (adj)   inspiring (adj)   inspiration (n)

   a. She played the piece as if _____.

   b. The author said that the story _____ by her experiences with homeless children during the war.

   c. The composer said that the folk music she had heard as a child provided the _____ for the work.

   d. His speech was so _____ that many people were persuaded to support his cause.

5. composer (n)   composition (n)   compose (v)

   a. The piece _____ for piano and violin.

   b. The _____ completed his last work shortly before his death.

   c. Redolfi's _____ include sounds heard from the depths of the sea.

6. revolution (n)   revolutionize (v)   revolutionary (adj, n)

   a. Computers have caused _____ changes in our lives.

   b. The historian's latest book is about the Russian _____.

   c. The invention of the telephone _____ communications.

   d. Thomas Paine was a famous American _____ .

7. participation (n)   participant (n)   participate (v)

   a. All _____ in the contest have been asked to arrive an hour early.

   b. Your _____ in the bake sale was greatly appreciated.

   c. The child refused to _____ in any of the games at the party.

8. visionary (n)   vision (n)   envision (v)

   a. How do you _____ your life ten years from now?

   b. The architect was a _____ whose ideas weren't accepted until many years after her death.

   c. In her latest novel, the author expresses her _____ of what life will be like in the future.

IV. Sentence Completion

Complete each sentence using one of the words listed below.

illusions   snorkel   resonated   frolic   microphone   murmur   trance   submerged

1.   We couldn't hear the speaker because the _____ wasn't working well.
2.   We lay on the beach watching the children _____ in the sand.
3.   She walked across the stage as if in a(n) _____ .
4.   During our hike, we stopped by a brook to rest; the only sound we heard was the soft _____ of running water.
5.   In 1989 the tanker Valdez hit _____ rocks near the coast of Alaska.
6.   He had no _____ about the difficulties he would face adjusting to life in a new country.
7.   Don't forget to bring your mask and _____ when we go to the beach.
8.   As she played, the rich sound of the instrument _____ throughout the room.

COUNTERPARTS

1. Making a Venn Diagram is a useful way to compare and contrast two things. In the overlapping areas of the circles in the diagram, tell how the two things are alike. In the outer areas, tell how they are different. Add ideas to the Venn Diagram below to compare and contrast an underwater concert and a traditional concert.

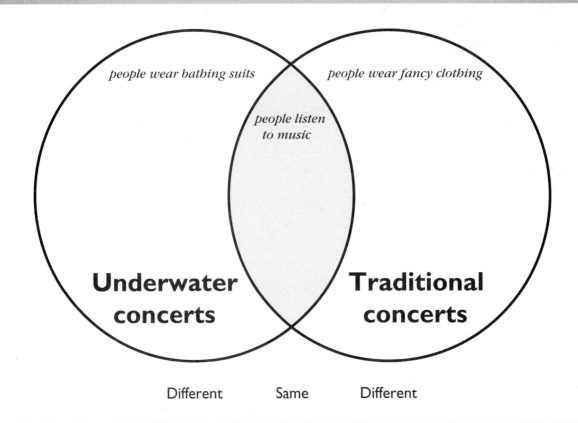

people wear bathing suits

people wear fancy clothing

people listen to music

Underwater concerts

Traditional concerts

Different   Same   Different

Use the information in your Venn Diagram to write a paragraph comparing and contrasting these two kinds of concerts.

2. Redolfi believes that avant-garde music needs an equally avant-garde environment. The underwater world is one example of an avant-garde environment. What are some others? In a small group, list your ideas. Then choose one of the environments on your list and select the music you would provide at a concert in that environment. Describe your concert to the class.

3. Redolfi notes that many of his colleagues think he is some kind of "California nut." This is not surprising for new ideas are often greeted with skepticism. Can you think of other ideas in art and science that were not immediately accepted?

4. Describe a concert that you attended. Include information about both the environment and the music.

Citizenship: A Difficult Choice

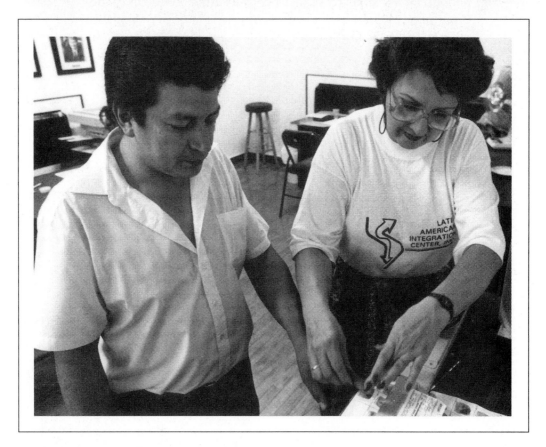

"If people like me retain our allegiances to home and refuse to participate in electoral politics here," said Armando Espinosa, an immigrant from Ecuador, "the lot of our race will never improve." He was fingerprinted by Amparo Aristizibel for a citizenship application at Latin American Integration Center.

1. Of what country are you a citizen? For what reasons, if any, would you become a citizen of another country?

2. What difficult decisions do immigrants to a new country have to make?

3. What do you think this chapter is about? Scan the article for one minute. Then share ideas with your classmates.

or most of his 12 years in this country, Armando Espinosa, an immigrant from Ecuador, had no intention of becoming a United States citizen. What would be the purpose? he asked himself. With a green card in his wallet, he led a comfortable life in New York, working as an industrial mechanic while his two children flourished° in public schools. He certainly did not consider himself American.

did well

"I am Ecuadorean in my blood and my gut,°" he said. "I do not even like apple pie."

stomach; insides

Mr. Espinosa was hardly alone in his thinking. Unlike 50 years ago, when the majority of immigrants routinely decided to naturalize,° only slightly more than a third of legal permanent residents now apply to become citizens. Although advocates for immigrants believe that the tide is turning,° most immigrants now exist in a state of legal limbo,° many nourished by the dream, often an illusion, that they will someday return home.

become a citizen of a country

tide is turning: things are changing/a state of uncertainty

Numbering up to 10 million nationally, these immigrants form a growing population of tax-paying residents. But they do not have the right to vote or to serve on juries,° police forces, or in many federal jobs.

groups of people who make decisions in a court of law

Legal immigrants are eligible for citizenship after five years in the United States, or after three years if they are married to a citizen. The reasons that most do not naturalize are complex, ranging from their close ties to home in the age of jet travel and long-distance telephone calls to their fear of the citizenship interview—in which immigration officials may ask them to "Name the order in which the 13 colonies came into the union" or "Explain the stripes on the American flag."

"It's easier to exist in limbo between two worlds," said Margie McHugh, executive director of the New York Immigration Coalition. "Because people can come and go more easily, they are not forced to make the ultimate choice of where they want to pledge their allegiance."°

pledge their allegiance: promise their loyalty

Mr. Espinosa's attitude toward citizenship slowly evolved. As his children—one born in the United States—became Americanized, he found himself increasingly interested in the laws and politics of his new country. He could no longer vote in

Ecuador and he could not vote in the United States. He began to feel like a man without a nation, he said.

Slowly angered by what he saw as the political weakness of Hispanic residents, Mr. Espinosa said he felt guilty. "If people like me retain our allegiances to home and refuse to participate in electoral politics° here," he said, "the lot° of our race will never improve."

Because immigration is at peak° levels, the numbers of legal immigrants who apply for citizenship are still substantial, about 300,000 a year. But the proportions° are low. About 37 percent apply for citizenship, compared with about 67 percent in 1946, according to Immigration and Naturalization Service statistics.

Immigrants who find it harder to return home for visits—political refugees° and those who come from farther away are likeliest to become citizens. Vietnamese refugees are eight times as likely to naturalize as economic migrants from Canada, for instance.

"You have to understand that many immigrants feel lost and diminished° when they come to this country," said Saramaria Archila, a Colombian immigrant and executive director of the Latin American Integration Center. "What they have left is their national identity, and they are loath to give that up."

Lucia Alvarez, a Guatemalan immigrant who works for the city's Human Resources Administration, said that after 13 years in this country the decision to become a citizen was a troubling one despite her gratitude toward the United States.

"I feel bad, torn, toward my country, as if I'm abandoning it," Ms. Alvarez said. "It's like denying something about yourself."

Still, as a citizen, Ms. Alvarez will be able to sponsor° her mother to join her in this country without the difficulties she has experienced for years.

"There's no turning back° now, I guess," Ms. Alvarez said, as she sealed the envelope with her photos, her fingerprints and the details of her life and character.

electoral politics: voting/ situation; way of life

the highest

a part compared to the whole

people who are forced to leave their countries

made to feel smaller or unimportant

take responsibility for

turning back: changing plans

This chart shows the steps from green card to citizenship in the United States:

The Route to Citizenship

Immigrants with green cards (legal permanent residents) who are 18 or older are eligible to apply for citizenship after living in the United States for five years, or after three years if married to a citizen. Green-card holders are entitled to many of the benefits available to citizens — for example, they are eligible for public assistance (unemployment compensation and medicare). But they can't do everything a citizen can. Here are some of the key distinctions, and a brief summary of the steps to naturalization.

BENEFITS OF CITIZENSHIP: **Citizens can vote,** serve on juries and qualify for all Government jobs; green-card holders can't.

Citizens travel freely; green-card holders are subject to time limits on travel abroad.

Citizens can sponsor more relatives entering the United States (green-card holders can't sponsor parents or siblings); citizens' relatives are processed faster.

NATURALIZATION: The steps from green card to citizenship

❶ PHOTOGRAPHS
Have three color photographs taken.

❷ FINGERPRINTS
Have fingerprints taken at a police station, sheriff's office, immigration office, commercial shop or immigrant community center.

❸ APPLICATION
Fill out the four-page Immigration and Naturalization Service application for U.S. citizenship. Its questions cover residential and employment history, marital status, military service, and criminal record, if any. It also contains questions about politics and character. For example:
• Have you ever been a habitual drunkard?
• Have you ever been a member of the Communist Party?
• Have you ever practiced polygamy?

❹ MAIL FORM AND FEE
Enclose a $90 fee with the application; mail to I.N.S.

Expect to wait several months to receive an interview date.

❺ PREPARE FOR EXAM
As an alternative to taking an English and civics test at the interview, take the standardized Educational Testing Service exam at an immigrant agency, for a $16 fee. Sample questions:
• During the Civil War, the President was . . . ?
• Where were the original 13 colonies?

❻ INTERVIEW
Report to interview. Bring documents to support application information.

❼ SWEARING-IN
If you pass, report to a swearing-in ceremony (in New York, it will be a month or two after the exam).

Source: Immigration and Naturalization Service

Megan Jaegerman/The New York Times

entitled: have the right
benefits: money and services provided by the government
distinctions: differences
siblings: sisters and brothers
drunkard: someone who often drinks a lot of alcohol
polygamy: having more than one wife or husband at the same time

EXERCISES

I.   Comprehension and Discussion Questions

General Ideas
1.   What is the main idea of the third paragraph of the article?
2.   According to the article, why do fewer immigrants become U.S. citizens today than in the past?

3. How do Mr. Espinosa and Ms. Alvarez feel about becoming U.S. citizens? In what ways are their attitudes the same and different?

Details
4. Scan the reading to find answers to the questions below.
    a. What is Armando Espinosa's occupation?
    b. How many legal immigrants are there in the U.S. today?
    c. When can a legal immigrant apply for citizenship?
    d. How many people apply for citizenship each year?
    e. Where is Lucia Alvarez from?

Opinions
5. What do immigrants gain by becoming U.S. citizens? What do they lose?
6. Based on the sentence below, what role in electoral politics do you think Mr. Espinosa will take after he becomes a U.S. citizen?

    "If people like me retain our allegiances to home and refuse to participate in electoral politics here," Mr. Espinosa said, "the lot of our race will never improve."

7. What interested you most in this article? Why?

II. Vocabulary in Context

Use context to guess the meaning of the italicized words below. Then look up each word in a dictionary. Choose the dictionary definition that best fits the meaning of the word in this context.

1. For most of his 12 years in this country, Armando Espinosa had no *intention* of becoming a United States citizen. What would be the purpose? he asked himself. With a green card in his wallet, he led a comfortable life in New York.

    My guess: _____

    Dictionary definition: _____

2. Legal immigrants are *eligible* for citizenship after five years in the country, or after three years if they are married to a citizen.

    My guess: _____

    Dictionary definition: _____

3. Mr. Espinosa's attitude toward citizenship slowly *evolved*. As his children became American-ized, he found himself increasingly interested in the laws and politics of his new country.

    My guess: _____

    Dictionary definition: _____

4. "If people like me *retain* our allegiances to home and refuse to participate in electoral politics here," Mr. Espinosa said, "the lot of our race will never improve."

    My guess: _____

    Dictionary definition: _____

5. Because immigration is at peak levels, the numbers of legal immigrants who apply for citizen-ship are still *substantial*, about 300,000 a year.

    My guess: _____

    Dictionary definition: _____

6. "You have to understand that many immigrants feel lost and diminished when they come to this country," said Saramaria Archila. "What they have left is their national identity, and they are *loath* to give that up."

    My guess: _____

    Dictionary definition: _____

7. Lucia Alvarez, a Guatemalan immigrant, said that the decision to become a citizen was a troubling one despite her *gratitude* toward the United States.

    My guess: _____

    Dictionary definition: _____

III. Between the Lines

Choose the answer that best completes each of the following statements.

1. The main idea of the first paragraph is that
    a. Mr. Espinosa didn't like living in the United States.
    b. Mr. Espinosa did not have a reason for becoming a U.S. citizen.
    c. Mr. Espinosa was glad to be a U.S. citizen.

2. The main idea of the fifth paragraph is that
    a. most legal immigrants choose to naturalize.
    b. for a variety of reasons, many legal immigrants decide not to become citizens.
    c. immigration officials ask difficult questions.

3. The article gives the impression that the citizenship exam

    a. is easy.   b. is popular.   c. is difficult.

4. Which sentence best describes Mr. Espinosa's attitude towards voting?

    a. People with green cards shouldn't be able to vote.

    b. It doesn't matter if you vote.

    c. More people should vote.

5. According to the article, immigrants who _____ are less likely to become U.S. citizens.

    a. can't return home

    b. come from nearby countries

    c. have family members in the United States

6. Which statement best describes Lucia Alvarez's attitude towards becoming a U.S. citizen?

    a. I'm losing something but I'm gaining something, too.

    b. It was an easy decision to make.

    c. My main reason for becoming a U.S. citizen is so that I can vote.

IV. Word Forms

Put the correct form of the word in each blank. Check the verb forms for correct tense, number, and voice (active or passive), and check the nouns for number (singular or plural).

1. intention (n)   intend (v)   intentionally (adv)

    a. If you _____ to become a U.S. citizen, you must fill out an application form and take an exam.

    b. Despite the fact that her children were born in the United States, she has no _____ of becoming a U.S. citizen.

    c. I didn't make a mistake on the application form _____. I just wasn't thinking clearly.

2. immigrant (n)   immigrate (v)

    a. When my parents _____ to the United States, they couldn't speak English very well.

    b. About 300,000 _____ apply for citizenship each year.

3. nourishment (n)   nourish (v)

    Food is _____ for the body while ideas _____ the mind.

4. existence (n)   exist (v)   existing (adj)

    a. _____ immigration laws say that legal residents can become citizens after five years in the country.

    b. No law _____ that says immigrants must become citizens.

    c. The _____ of jets and telephones makes it easier for immigrants to maintain close ties to home.

5. application (n)   apply (v)

    a. When you fill out an _____ for U.S. citizenship, you must answer a number of questions.

    b. Immigrants with green cards can _____ for citizenship if they have lived in the United States for at least five years.

V.   Sentence Completion

Complete each sentence, using one of the words listed below.

    peaked   eligible   retain   diminishing   loath   refugees   limbo

1. I'm in _____ because I can't decide what to do.

2. My brother is _____ to become a citizen but he is going to wait a few more years.

3. The number of immigrants _____ this year. It's the highest number ever.

4. The amount of money in my bank account is _____. Soon I won't have any money left.

5. Although she is _____ to change her nationality, she thinks it is necessary.

6. War in the former Yugoslavia forced many people to become _____.

7. Holders of green cards don't have to become U.S. citizens. They can _____ their citizenship of birth.

COUNTERPARTS

1. In a small group, study the graph below. Does the information in this graph support the ideas in paragraph 10 of the article? How?

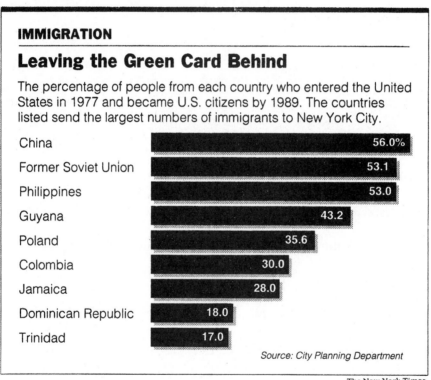

IMMIGRATION

Leaving the Green Card Behind

The percentage of people from each country who entered the United States in 1977 and became U.S. citizens by 1989. The countries listed send the largest numbers of immigrants to New York City.

Country	Percentage
China	56.0%
Former Soviet Union	53.1
Philippines	53.0
Guyana	43.2
Poland	35.6
Colombia	30.0
Jamaica	28.0
Dominican Republic	18.0
Trinidad	17.0

Source: City Planning Department

The New York Times

2. With a partner, list the advantages and disadvantages of becoming a U.S. citizen. Use information from the article as well as your own ideas.

Advantages	Disadvantages

Do the advantages outweigh the disadvantages? In other words, are the advantages more important? Share your answers with the class.

3. Describe the laws and procedures for becoming a citizen of a country other than the United States. Here are some questions you might answer:

  • Who can become a citizen?

  • How long does it take to become a citizen?

  • What do you have to do to become a citizen?

  • What would you gain by becoming a citizen?

4. To become a U.S. citizen, immigrants used to have to take an oral English and civics test. Today, however, people can choose to take a standardized written test. Why do you think this change was made? How might a standardized test be fairer?

About Men: Conflicting Interests

1. Think of someone you know who is a father. What role does this person take in raising his children? Tell a partner.

2. Read the title and study the pictures in this chapter. What is similar about these pictures?

3. Read the first sentence of each paragraph on page 33. Based on this information, what conflicting interests do you think this article will discuss?

hange is not easy, and many men have come to feel a good deal of anger and resentment in their lives. There is a sense that somehow they have been deprived° of the chance to become the sort of men they expected to be as they grew up—men who, like those of earlier generations, possess a sense of what is expected and of how to meet those expectations.

had something taken away

Contradictions increasingly rule our lives. On the one hand, a majority of people now believe that both sexes should enjoy equal employment opportunities. On the other, most also believe that children may be harmed psychologically if their mothers work outside the home. Says a prominent° researcher in this field, "One fundamental American value is that family and parenthood are important, and this belief is now being extended to include men to a much greater degree. This attitude contradicts the traditional belief, however, that a man should be mainly the breadwinner."°

well-known

one who earns money for family/pressure

The result can be considerable strain and tension.°

"It's really hard to balance my career against my role as a father and also to have some time left over for myself," says Fred Sherman, a Chicago-area lawyer. "I really resent those evenings when I have to stay late at the office and when I can't get home to see my wife and daughter, or when I have to get out early in the morning. I sometimes have to work six or seven days a week, and while I enjoy my job, I'm often upset° that it pulls me away from my family. It only takes two or three nights of working late and having to kiss my daughter after she's asleep to feel that I've really missed something important."

disturbed

One colleague° of mine, a history professor, seems successfully to combine his career with a family of three children. His wife, too, enjoys a highly productive academic career with the same rank and obligations. But the ability to pursue work and personal life comes at the price of time. "Occasionally, my wife and I both feel a sense of resentment about balancing two busy schedules," he says, "and sometimes we'll let each other know that we feel victimized by the requirements of the other partner. In order to make a go of° this sort of life, we have had to cut out almost everything that does not relate to family or career, and we often feel that we are up against the ropes° in

work associate

make a go of: succeed at

up against the ropes: pressured

focus on: center on, make clear

retreat/wounding remarks

raising

give one's full attention

following strictly

regard to the time available. Finally, it's the amenities of life in terms of friends, entertainment, and general leisure that gets put aside in order to focus on° the everyday essentials."

Dick Young, an Atlanta attorney, speaks of similar conflicts. "Although I am a pretty traditional person," he says, "my wife has her own career as a lawyer, and I've had to give up some of my traditional expectations. When I arrive home from a tough day, all I want to do is put my feet up and have a drink—the sort of thing that a man has always expected. Instead, I have to help with the household or attend to my children. As a consequence, I sometimes feel that I can't be fair both to my own needs and to those of my family."

My own wife now works more than forty hours a week, mostly in the afternoon and evening. As a result, I frequently must cut short my own work day in order to pick up our eighteen-month-old son from day care or spend time with my older child. Often, I am also the one who is on call in case of illness, who prepares many of the meals, and who keeps the house clean.

I have many fewer hours available for work than I wish, and sometimes I am too exhausted at the end of a day to resume my work when the children have gone to bed. I cannot pretend to feel comfortable about this, and at times I explode with rage or I withdraw° into sarcasm° and moodiness. There is no question that the rewards of sharing career achievement and child rearing° with one's spouse are great, but the price paid can be high. It is a price, finally, that many of us never imagined we would have to pay, and therein lies much of the trouble.

"I guess that in terms of work and family," says Nick Taylor, an Atlanta journalist whose spouse is a television reporter, "we are faced with having to become supermen in response to today's superwomen."

Maybe some of us might be able to do this. Maybe we might learn—in the words of my departmental colleague to give up the amenities of life in order to concentrate° on the essentials, adhering° not only to precise daily schedules but working late into the night (a major ingredient in the success of many men who seem able to combine the demands of work and family). We might, in addition, learn to take pride in the career attainments of our wives, even if we must sacrifice some of our own professional ambitions. We might find the time, as well, to be with our children and to be involved in the necessary household chores. We might even learn to give up the anger and resentment that is often generated by the need to do all of these things, and to do them well.

We might. But most of us, as yet, cannot hope to follow such a program, nor should we criticize ourselves if we do not live up to the "superman" image. Despite the things we did learn from our own fathers, we usually did not find out how to balance full participation in work and in family. Now we are exploring uncharted° territory, with all of the mistakes and false starts that such exploration requires.

unknown

finally

Still, if we think about it, we might ultimately° come to gain from the new requirements in our lives. On the morning I was to begin writing this, my eighteen-month-old son woke up with a fever. My wife had a full schedule at the office, and this sick child clearly could not go to his baby-sitter. The only solution was for me to alter my plans and to stay home, where I diapered,° played with, worried over, and comforted a still-energetic but cranky° baby. I could feel my bitterness and resentment boiling—for lost hours at work, for missed deadlines,° for unprepared classes. "Men today," I found myself thinking, "really have a bad deal."

put baby pants on
cross, upset
time when something must be finished

Then I discovered that my son had learned something new. For the first time, he was able to give a proper kiss. "Kees Dada," he said as he bussed° me on the nose and cheeks. No amount of gratification° at work could have compensated° for that moment. I found out another thing that morning. I suddenly realized that in sacrificing my work day, I had learned a lot about how fathers might care for their sons. And I found that I had learned something further about what it means to be a man, something that goes beyond simply bringing home a paycheck.

kissed
satisfaction/paid back

EXERCISES

I.   Comprehension and Discussion Questions

General Ideas

1. How are the lives of many married men today different from the way they were thirty years ago?

2. What are some of the problems these men face, both at home and in their careers?

3. What is the main idea of this article?

Details

4. What do you know about the writer of this article? Scan the article to find answers to the questions below.

    a. Does his wife work?

    b. How many children does he have?

    c. What role does he take in raising his children?

Opinions

5. What advice do you think the writer of this article would give to a new father?

6. Reread the last sentence of the article. What do you think the writer means?

7. Do you think it is possible for a husband and wife to share the responsibilities of child rearing equally? Why or why not?

II.   Between the Lines

Choose the answer that completes each of the following statements.

1. The main idea of the second paragraph is that
    a. there are many contradictions in life.
    b. mothers shouldn't have full-time jobs.
    c. traditional values often conflict with current beliefs.

2. The author of this article is probably a
    a. college professor.
    b. businessman.
    c. lawyer.

3. The history professor interviewed in the article says that to successfully combine a career and family, he has had to make sacrifices in which one of these areas?
    a. finances
    b. outside interests
    c. marriage

4. Which of the following statements would Dick Young probably agree with?
    a. Women shouldn't have careers.
    b. Men shouldn't do household chores.
    c. Men had easier lives in the past.

5. Most of the people interviewed in this article are
    a. working class.
    b. upper middle class.
    c. independently wealthy.

6. The main idea of the last paragraph is that
    a. work is less important than family life.
    b. it isn't necessary for the husband to be the sole "breadwinner."
    c. child rearing can be a highly rewarding experience for men.

III.   Vocabulary in Context

Use context to choose the word or term that best fits the meaning of the italicized words in the sentences below. Circle your answers.

1.   "I sometimes have to work six or seven days a week, and *while* I enjoy my work, I'm often upset that it pulls me away from my family."

   a.   when   b.   perhaps   c.   although

2.   "It's the *amenities* of life, in terms of friends, entertainment, and general leisure that get put aside in order to concentrate on everyday essentials."

   a.   enjoyable things   b.   difficult things   c.   necessary things

3.   I have many fewer hours available for work than I wish, and sometimes I am too exhausted at the end of the day to *resume* my work when the children have gone to bed.

   a.   find   b.   continue   c.   put away

4.   There is no question that the rewards of sharing career achievement and child rearing with one's *spouse* are great, but the price paid can be high.

   a.   children   b.   parents   c.   husband or wife

5.   We might even learn to give up the anger and resentment that is often *generated* by the need to do all of these things, and to do them well.

   a.   caused   b.   enjoyed   c.   lost

6.   On the morning I was to begin writing this, my eighteen-month-old son woke up with a fever. My wife had a full schedule at the office, and this sick child clearly could not go to his baby-sitter. The only solution was for me to *alter* my plans and to stay home.

   a.   follow   b.   change   c.   give

IV.   Word Forms

Put the correct form of the word in each blank. Check the verb forms for correct tense, number, and voice (active or passive), and check the nouns for number (singular or plural).

1.   deprivation (n)   deprive (v)   deprived (adj)

   a.   The journalist wrote of the disease and _____ that he had witnessed in the war-torn country.

   b.   Prisoners _____ of their freedom to come and go.

   c.   She is the director of a camp for _____ children.

2. expectation (n)   expect (v)

    a. He felt that he had never lived up to his father's _____.

    b. I _____ to see him yesterday, but he never showed up.

3. psychology (n)   psychologist (n)   psychological (adj)

    a. He used to work for a _____ testing service.

    b. The subject of the paper was related to animal _____.

    c. The _____ studied the effect of high noise levels on people who live in big cities.

4. researcher (n)   research (n, v)

    a. The professor suggested that I _____ the problem more carefully.

    b. After completing his _____, he published a paper on his findings.

    c. The news program had several _____ on its staff.

5. victim (n)   victimize (v)

    a. She felt that she _____ because of her religious beliefs.

    b. The detective noticed that all of the murderer's _____ had been red-headed men between the ages of twenty-five and thirty.

6. gratification (n)   gratify (v)   gratified (adj)   gratifying (adj)

    a. The couple were _____ by the enormous response to their appeal for help.

    b. The author said that the success of his first novel was very _____.

    c. The grandmother was quick to _____ the child's every wish.

    d. The old man said that today's youth was always seeking instant _____, rather than working long and hard for material rewards, as his generation had done.

7. exhaustion (n)   exhaust (v)   exhausted (adj)   exhausting (adj)

    a. The ten-hour plane ride was _____.

    b. We were so _____ that we fell asleep in the taxi on the way to the hotel.

    c. Because we hadn't exercised in months, that hike up the mountain _____ us.

    d. _____ and mental strain finally caused him to change his lifestyle.

8. sarcasm (n)   sarcastic (adj)

    a. He was offended by her _____ reply.

    b. Her _____ amused some people and annoyed others.

V.   Sentence Completion

Complete each sentence using one of the words listed below.

anticipate   deadline   prominent   spouse   cranky   fundamentals   rage   tension

1. This legal document must be signed by both you and your _____. Could you please ask your wife to sign it too?

2. He became a(n) _____ figure in the field of international law by writing numerous articles for well-known journals.

3. If you haven't studied the _____ of physics, you should take an introductory course.

4. She left the room in a(n) _____, slamming the door behind her.

5. By the end of the long bus ride, the child sitting in front of me had become very _____.

6. In order to meet the _____, I had to stay up all night writing.

7. There was enormous _____ in the courtroom as the judge began to speak.

8. His behavior is very unpredictable. I can't _____ what he will do.

COUNTERPARTS

1. An increasing number of women in the United States are joining the work force. Is this also true in your native country? If so, how has this change affected the roles of a husband and wife?

2. Interview someone you know who is a parent. Find out what this person likes and dislikes about being a parent. Report what you learned to the class.

3. In your opinion, what are the responsibilities of parents? With your classmates, add to the list in the chart below.

Responsibilities of parents	Mother only	Father only	Both mother and father
Take care of children when they are sick			
Feed the children			
Discipline the children			
Spend time with the children			
Keep the house clean			

Do mothers and fathers have the same responsibilities? Explore this question in small groups. Use a checkmark (✔) to record your group's ideas in the chart. Then compare charts with another group.

An Alternative: Mothers Who Return Home

1. Do you know any women who have both young children and full-time jobs? Do you think mothers with young children should work? Why or why not?

2. Read the title of this chapter. What do you think this article is about?

3. Read the first two paragraphs of the article. If you were writing this article, what questions would you ask women who have stopped working to raise their children? List your questions. Then, read the article to look for answers to your questions.

A lot has been said about the so-called Supermom,° the woman who tries to juggle° a career with a family. As Supermom struggles to do it all, another group of women have come to the conclusion that the pressures of this dual° role can often cause them to be mediocre° at both.

So they have given up their careers to stay home with their children.

"It seems to me that this is the way the pendulum is swinging,"° said Buffy McKay, thirty years old, who left her job as a managing clerk in a Manhattan law firm when her daughter, Frances, now six weeks old, was born. "Women are no longer afraid to say that they're quitting their jobs for a while, or for a long time." Asked why she thought this was so, she replied: "Maybe it's because a great number of women have achieved success. Everyone's accepted the fact that women have careers. It's not a big deal° anymore."

Some of the women who have left careers view their new role of homemaker as permanent; others view it as a temporary solution until their children start school; still others are not sure whether they want to return to work. Whatever their situation, they are not alone in staying home. According to the Bureau of Labor Statistics, 41.6 percent of women with children under age six are not in the labor force.

One area where former career women are virtually° all in agreement is that they have had to make major changes in their style of living now that they are forced to get by on their husbands' salaries alone.

"My husband and I don't go out as much," said Ann Grube, thirty-one years old, of Manhattan, who quit her job as an assistant vice-president of a bank after her daughter, Kate, now eight months old, was born.

"When you go out, not only do you have to buy tickets, you also have to pay a baby-sitter,° which is one of the most expensive things in New York City."

Leslie Schaeffer, thirty-six, a former public-relations executive, who is at home in Manhattan with her two young daughters, put the money situation this way: "I hate asking my husband for money. I liked having my own checking account." Most of the women, though, feel that the rewards they get from

---

extraordinary mother
do several things at a time

double/neither good nor bad

pendulum is swinging:
   direction things are going

big deal: *important*

essentially

one who takes care of children

raising their children are far greater than the financial rewards of high-paying careers. "A baby grows up so quickly," said Joyce Coleman, thirty-four, of the Bronx, who was a secretary and a manager of a large company in Manhattan for five years before her second son, Jared, three months, was born. "Something interesting happens almost everyday—his first smile, the first time he recognizes people," she said. "If I were working I feel I'd miss all that."

Asked what had been her most memorable experience as a mother in the home, Mrs. Coleman smiled and told about the time she took cake, toys, and balloons to her son Christopher's school in honor of his third birthday. "I got the nicest long note back from his teacher," she said. "She thanked me for taking the time to do it. If I had been working, I couldn't have done something like that."

Mrs. Grube said she had been inspired to stay home by the example of her mother, who raised four children. "I just knew I couldn't both do my job and raise my child well," she explained. "I had always given myself so totally to whatever I had done, and I knew I couldn't give myself 100 percent to my child and keep my marriage."

She and several other mothers pointed out that even if they had continued working, the cost of full-time baby-sitters for their children would have used up a large portion of their income.

Most of the women who were interviewed said that occasionally it got boring around the house when one's only conversational partner could only speak baby talk. So several of the women have adopted ways of coping. Mrs. Grube has what she calls a sanity° day every Monday, when a baby-sitter stays with her daughter so she can pursue other interests. She is active in the New York Junior League, where she is a chairman of the English-teaching committee for the foreign-born, and in fund-raising activities for her alma mater,° Stanford University.

"If you don't have something else to do besides sit, feed your child, and play with your child, you're going to go crazy," she said. "I think that's why women become volunteers."°

Leslie Schaeffer says that she began to run after she began to feel stir-crazy.° She gets up at 6 A.M. almost every day and runs five or six miles. She has competed in two New York City Marathons,° finishing 256th among 1,251 women in a half-marathon in Central Park. "It gives me a feeling of achievement that I don't get otherwise," she said.

good mental health

alma mater: where one studied

those who work without pay

very restless

long races

Vivian Toan, a thirty-five-year-old lawyer who quit her job to stay home with her three children, said she spent her spare hours doing things she was unable to do while working—gardening, knitting, reading, and carpentry. She said that one summer she took the children to Colorado, where she rebuilt an old garage that she and her husband, Robert, a lawyer, use for hiking° in summer and skiing° in winter.

walking long distances/sport, sliding over snow

"I enjoy my life so much," she said. "I know a lot of women feel a sense of social pressure that this is an old-fashioned lifestyle, and they're embarrassed° or guilty about not working. I felt a little like that myself, but now I'm fairly confident that I've done the right thing."

felt uncomfortable

The major worry for most is that if they do decide to go back to work they will have difficulty finding jobs. "The longer you're out, the harder it is to get a job," Mrs. Toan said. "A lot of

frightening dream

doctor who treats mental problems

keep, preserve

lawyers are suspicious when you've been out of a job for several years. I think it's going to be very hard when I go back." Mrs. Schaeffer put it this way: "I have a nightmare° about going back to my old office, and nobody knows who I am and they don't have any time for me. That's true anxiety, and you don't have to be a psychiatrist° to know it."

Several of the women said they continued to read in their fields so that they would not fall too far behind. Others said that they tried to have lunch occasionally with former co-workers to keep up with what was going on.

"That's the most important thing—to maintain° contacts with your colleagues in the working world," Mrs. Coleman said. "Otherwise you feel that you're not connected with the work. You feel that you're a bit out of touch."

On the other hand, she and several other women reported that they were surprised to find that they were not as homebound as they thought they would be.

"You'd be amazed how many things you discover when you walk around the neighborhood with your kids," Mrs. Coleman said. "I discovered the local public library, which has puppet° shows, and a playground with a kiddie pool."°

doll with movable parts/**kiddie pool:** place for young children to swim

Mrs. McKay added, "That was one of my fears—lack of adult companionship. But it was not a problem. Most of the women I know have given up careers or jobs and are at home with their children."

EXERCISES

I.   Comprehension and Discussion Questions

General Ideas

1.   What is the main idea of the fourth paragraph in the reading?

2.   When women stop working and become full-time mothers, how does their lifestyle change?

3.   What reasons do the women in the article give for leaving the work force to become full-time homemakers?

4.   What do these women do to avoid getting bored in their roles as full-time homemakers?

Details

5.   Scan the article to find information to complete the chart below.

Name	Age	Occupation	Thoughts about being a full-time homemaker
Ann Grube			
Leslie Schaeffer			
Joyce Coleman			
Vivian Toan			

Opinions

6.   Think about the occupations of the women mentioned in the article. In what way are their occupations alike? Do you think this article represents the ideas of most women? Why or why not?

7.   Many women cannot choose to stay at home. They have to work because their families need the money. How do you think these women might respond to the article?

II.   Between the Lines

Choose the answer that completes each of the following statements and questions.

1.   A Supermom is a woman who

   a.   has given up her career to stay home and take care of her child.

   b.   has tried to be both a successful career woman and a mother.

   c.   has decided to devote all her energy to furthering her career.

2. Most of the women interviewed left their careers to take care of their children because

    a. they were bored with their jobs.

    b. they no longer felt that they had to prove that women can have successful careers.

    c. they didn't believe that they could be successful as both career women and mothers.

3. The important change in their lifestyle after leaving their jobs came as a result of

    a. facing the challenge of being a responsible parent.

    b. trying to pay the bills on a reduced budget.

    c. having to ask their husbands for money.

4. Vivian Toan believes that many women who have given up their careers to stay home feel "embarrassed or guilty" because

    a. their husbands must pay for all the household expenses.

    b. it is considered old-fashioned to be a full-time homemaker.

    c. they can do only volunteer work.

5. Many women who have left the work force do volunteer work because

    a. the work is easy.

    b. these women have no financial pressures.

    c. they occasionally feel bored at home.

6. Most of the women interviewed in the article are

    a. poor.   b. single mothers.   c. well educated.

7. Which of the following statements would most of the women interviewed probably *disagree* with?

    a. The rewards of being a full-time parent far outweigh its disadvantages.

    b. A woman who has had the opportunity to be a full-time mother would never want to return to the work force.

    c. Women can be as successful as men in their careers.

III. Vocabulary in Context

Use context to choose the word or term that best fits the meaning of the italicized words in the sentences below. Circle your answers.

1. One area where former career women are virtually all in agreement is that they have had to make major changes in their style of living now that they are forced to *get by on* their husbands' salaries alone.

    a. add to   b. live on   c. double

2. Asked what has been her most *memorable* experience as a mother in the home, Mrs. Cole-man smiled and told about the time she took cake, toys, and balloons to her son Christopher's school in honor of his third birthday.

   a. special in some way   b. unhappiest   c. forgettable

3. Mrs. Grube and several other mothers pointed out that even if they had continued working, the cost of full-time baby-sitters for their children would have *used up* a large portion of their income.

   a. added to   b. made   c. cost

4. Most of the women said that occasionally it got boring around the house. So several of the women have adopted ways of *coping.* Mrs. Grube has what she calls a sanity day every Monday, when a baby-sitter stays with her daughter so she can pursue other interests.

   a. dealing with something   b. getting rid of something   c. playing with something

5. Leslie Schaeffer has competed in two New York City Marathons, finishing 256th among 1,251 women in the most recent half-marathon in Central Park. "It gives me a feeling of *achievement* that I don't get otherwise," she said.

   a. unhappiness   b. boredom   c. success

6. "I have a nightmare about going back to my old office, and nobody knows who I am and they don't have any time for me. That's true *anxiety,* and you don't have to be a psychiatrist to know it."

   a. fear and worry   b. pleasure   c. lack of success

IV. Word Forms

Put the correct form of the word in each blank. Check the verb forms for correct tense, number, and voice (active or passive), and check the nouns for number (singular or plural).

1. baby-sitter (n)   baby-sit (v)

   a. When I was in high school, I used to _____ on weekends to earn extra money.

   b. When we go out for the evening, we usually spend about $20 for a _____.

2. conclusion (n)   conclude (v)   conclusive (adj)

   a. After much discussion, the board of directors came to the _____ that the company should move out of the state.

   b. The governor _____ her speech with a plea that the city support her tax reform bill.

   c. The detective had no _____ evidence that the accused man had committed the crime.

3. marriage (n)   marry (v)   get married (verb phrase)   married (adj.)

    a. The current tax laws favor _____ people.

    b. Do you think it's necessary for the husband to earn more than the wife in order for a _____ to be successful?

    c. She soon realized that her husband _____ her for her money.

    d. The young couple _____ without their parent's approval.

4. solution (n)   solve (v)

    a. I worked on the math problem for an hour before _____ it.

    b. We spent many hours trying to find a _____ to the problem.

5. sanity (n)   sane (adj)

    a. "Exercise keeps me _____," the runner told reporters after he had won the marathon.

    b. To preserve my _____ during that difficult period, I often took long walks along the beach.

6. maintenance (n)   maintain (v)

    a. We must improve the _____ of city streets; they are filled with potholes.

    b. It became so expensive to _____ the old house that we decided to sell it.

7. anxiety (n)   anxious (adj)   anxiously (adv)

    a. We _____ awaited his reply.

    b. He suffered enormous _____ whenever he had to write a paper.

    c. She was _____ to find out the results of the exam.

8. reward (n, v)   rewarding (adj)

    a. She offered a _____ to anyone who could find her lost dog.

    b. Working with children can be a _____ experience.

    c. After the monkey had performed the trick, its trainer _____ it with some food.

COUNTERPARTS

1. The women in the article left the work force to become full-time mothers. Do many women with children work full time in your country? What are their reasons for working? Like the women mentioned in the article, do they have the option of becoming full-time mothers?

2. In 1983, Buffy McKay said, "It seems to me that this [women giving up their careers to stay home with their children] is the way the pendulum is swinging." In other words, McKay thought that more and more women would be returning home to become full-time homemakers. The following graph gives the statistics on the percentage of working women with young children. In a small group, study this information and tell if you think it supports McKay's prediction. Report your group's answer to the class.

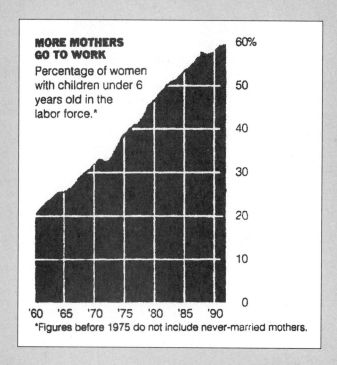

MORE MOTHERS GO TO WORK

Percentage of women with children under 6 years old in the labor force.*

*Figures before 1975 do not include never-married mothers.

3. Many women have to work because their families need the money. These women don't have the choice of becoming full-time mothers. What do you think are the most important things for these women to do with their children during the time they have available? What can they do to ensure that their children are well taken care of?

4. Many American women now delay having their first child until they are in their thirties. Do you think that these women make more capable parents than those who have children when they are teenagers or in their twenties? Give reasons to support your answer.

Elderhostel: Active Life After Age 60

1. Think of a retired person you know—someone who has stopped working because of his or her age. What does this person do during the day?

2. A hostel is a place where people can live and eat inexpensively. What do you think an elderhostel is?

3. Study the pictures in this chapter. What do they have in common? Based on these pictures, what do you think the article is about? Make a prediction.

hen Lenora Young retired from her career as a school administrator, she immediately retreated to the Virgin Islands for what she thought would be an idyllic° life. "At first it was delightful," Young recalls. "But before long, I got 'island fever' and started looking for something to do!"

delightful, charming

That "something" turned out to be a trip to Alaska to take a course in natural history and Native Alaskan culture, held at Tanana Community College and sponsored° by Elderhostel, a non-profit organization specializing in educational opportunities for older adults. "It was terrific," Young says of her first Elderhostel experience. "Ordinarily, I would never have attempted to travel to Alaska on my own. But going through a program like Elderhostel gave my trip a purpose. Knowing that I would be welcomed by a friendly group of classmates when I got there made my travels worry-free. As a woman traveling alone, I find this to be a wonderful thing."

organized

Many others have found Elderhostel to be a wonderful experience too. Last year, 250,000 older learners from the U.S. and Canada—retired° and semi-retired, female and male, couples and singles—ventured to campuses around the world to take part in a mindboggling° choice of studies in the liberal arts° and sciences sponsored by Elderhostel.

no longer working because of age

unbelievable
liberal arts: general education

For 18 years, the Boston-based organization has offered thousands of educational opportunities to people over the age of 60. Based on the youth hostels and folk° schools of Europe, the program combines two main elements—education and inexpensive lodgings°—to create a low-cost learning adventure at more than 1,900 colleges, universities, and other educational institutions. Currently there are host institutions° in all 50 states, the Canadian provinces, and in 47 countries overseas.

traditional

places to live and eat

host institution: an institution such as a university that makes its facilities available to guests

With Elderhostel, active seniors take short-term, non-credit residential courses at a host institution. In groups of 30-40, Elderhostelers live on the host campus—or in nearby hotels or inns—and take daily classes on a subject of their choice. Busy as they are during an Elderhostel program, participants need not worry about academic performance. Elderhostel professors assign no homework, nor are there any exams or grades. Programs are designed to promote° learning for the fun of it.

encourage

The variety of Elderhostel programs seems limitless. Depending on the location and nature° of the institution, Elderhostel students can learn about the music and folklore of Appalachia, receive a hands-on introduction to computers, study and compare the world's major religions, and gaze at stars through a telescope in an astronomy class. There are also courses in theater, ecology, history, and hundreds of other subjects.

Elderhostel's underlying° philosophy is that learning is a lifelong process which keeps the mind alert and active. Older adults, regardless of whether they finished high school or earned a college degree, benefit from the stimulation° of group discussions, new knowledge, and the exchange of ideas. The courses are designed to be introductory, requiring no prior° knowledge or formal training in the subject. Yet, the curriculum is challenging enough to appeal to individuals who have accumulated° 60+ years of life experience and opinions.

"Elderhostel is a great way to exercise the brain cells," claims Laura Kirven. Kirven, 74, was forced to put aside her personal interests and formal post-high school education as she raised four children by herself. "After my youngest daughter had her college diploma in hand, I said, 'Now I am ready to retire,'" laughs Kirven. "It was time to move on and do things for myself that I had to forgo° earlier. I needed to feed my mind."

Kirven began her "retirement" by taking seminars° in law and anthropology, and soon discovered Elderhostel. "I did it because I wanted to see if I could sit in a classroom and absorb what was being taught, without being distracted by other thoughts and concerns—Did I put the laundry in the dryer? Did I put dinner in the oven for the kids?—I found that I could, and my years of life experience more than made up for any lack of classroom experience." Kirven found that not only could she sit in a classroom, but that she could also participate fully and contribute to the lively class discussions and debates that are part of the Elderhostel experience.

Elderhostel offers seniors mental stimulation, physical adventure, friendship, and the opportunity to explore new places and new ideas. The modest° cost makes it exceptionally accessible:° a typical one-week program in the United States costs about $295, including lodging, meals, classes, and course-related field trips. The only restriction for participating in an Elderhostel program is age. Eligibility° begins at age 60, although a younger spouse° may attend with an age-eligible individual.

Glossary (margin):

type — *nature°*

basic — *underlying°*

excitement — *stimulation°*

previous — *prior°*

collected — *accumulated°*

give up — *forgo°*

small classes of students studying advanced subjects — *seminars°*

reasonable — *modest°*

easy to enter — *accessible:°*

the right to participate — *Eligibility°*

husband or wife — *spouse°*

With more people reaching their retirement years than ever before, there is a growing demand by older adults for meaningful activities and exciting new adventures. As Lenora Young concludes, "Retirement doesn't mean that you withdraw from life. It's really an opportunity to pursue new interests and open new doors."

EXERCISES

I.   Comprehension and Discussion Questions

General Ideas
1.   What is the purpose of Elderhostel?
2.   In what ways is attending an Elderhostel course different from taking a trip on your own?
3.   What is the main idea of the sixth paragraph in the reading?

Details
4.   Scan the reading to find answers to the questions below.

   a.   How old is the Elderhostel program?

   b.   Where do people live while taking an Elderhostel class?

   c.   How many people took Elderhostel classes last year?

   d.   How old do you have to be to take one of these classes?

   e.   How much does a typical one-week class cost?

Opinions
5.   Do you think the Elderhostel program is valuable? Why or why not?
6.   All of the people quoted in this article are women. Why do you think this is so?
7.   Would the Elderhostel program appeal to retired people in your culture? Why or why not?

II.   Vocabulary in Context

Use context to guess the meaning of the italicized words below. Then look up each word in a dictionary. Choose the definition that best fits the meaning of the word in this context.

1.   After she retired, Lenora Young moved to the Virgin Islands. "At first it was delightful," Young recalls. "But before long, I got *'island fever'* and started looking for something to do!"

   My guess: _____

   Dictionary definition: _____

2.   The variety of Elderhostel programs seems *limitless.* There are courses in theater, ecology, history, and hundreds of other subjects.

   My guess: _____

   Dictionary definition: _____

3. Elderhostel students can learn about the music of Appalachia, study and compare the world's major religions, and *gaze at* stars through a telescope in an astronomy class.

    My guess: _____

    Dictionary definition: _____

4. Elderhostel courses are designed to be *introductory,* requiring no prior knowledge or formal training in the subject.

    My guess: _____

    Dictionary definition: _____

5. Laura Kirven was forced to *put aside* her personal interests and formal post-high school education as she raised four children by herself.

    My guess: _____

    Dictionary definition: _____

6. "I wanted to take an Elderhostel course to see if I could sit in a classroom and absorb what was being taught, without being *distracted* by other thoughts and concerns—Did I put the laundry in the dryer? Did I put dinner in the oven for the kids?"

    My guess: _____

    Dictionary definition: _____

7. "Retirement doesn't mean that you withdraw from life. It's really an opportunity to *pursue* new interests and open new doors."

    My guess: _____

    Dictionary definition: _____

III. Finding the Facts: True or False?

Read each of the following statements and write *T* if the statement is true and *F* if it's false.

_____ 1. Elderhostel students can take classes at educational institutions in many countries.

_____ 2. A typical Elderhostel program costs $295 a week, which includes the cost of transportation to and from the host institution.

_____ 3. A 58-year-old woman cannot attend Elderhostel programs unless she goes with a husband who is 60 or older.

_____ 4. Laura Kirven had a college degree when she raised her four children.

_____ 5. Older students can work towards a college degree by taking Elderhostel classes.

_____ 6. You have to be rich to take Elderhostel classes.

_____ 7.   Grades are an important part of Elderhostel classes.

_____ 8.   You don't have to have a college degree to take Elderhostel courses.

Rewrite the false statements to make them true.

IV.   Between the Lines

Which of these conclusions can you draw from the information in the reading?

1.   Lenora Young decided to leave the Virgin Islands because she didn't have any friends there.

2.   Taking an Elderhostel course is a good way to meet new people.

3.   If you hate tests, you shouldn't take an Elderhostel course.

4.   You must be a U.S. citizen to take Elderhostel courses.

5.   Women are more likely than men to take Elderhostel courses.

6.   In the future, there will be a greater need for programs like Elderhostel.

V.   Word Forms

Put the correct form of the word in each blank. Check the verb forms for correct tense, number, and voice (active or passive), and check the nouns for number (singular or plural).

1.   retirement (n)   retire (v)   retired (adj)

    a. _____ people often have more time to travel than people who are still working.

    b. My father looks forward to _____ because there are a lot of things he wants to pursue.

    c. At what age do you plan to _____?

2.   organization (n)   organize (v)

    a. Elderhostel is a non-profit _____ which has its main office in Boston, Massachusetts.

    b. It takes a lot of work to _____ classes at different host institutions around the world.

3. resident (n)   reside (v)   residential (adj)

   a. If you want to live in a house rather than an apartment, you should look for a place to live in one of the _____ areas surrounding the city.

   b. For the first 15 years of her life, she _____ in a small town in the country.

   c. The _____ of my apartment building come from many different countries.

4. introduction (n)   introduce (v)   introductory (adj)

   a. If you don't know anything about astronomy, you should take an _____ course first.

   b. When I was a child, my father bought a small telescope so that he could _____ me to astronomy.

   c. He received an _____ to computers when he took a basic hands-on course at a community college.

5. stimulation (n)   stimulate (v)   stimulating (adj)

   a. It was a _____ course because it really made you think.

   b. Everyone can benefit from the _____ of new ideas and interesting discussion.

   c. For many people, taking courses _____ the mind; it's a good way to stay active and alert.

6. accumulation (n)   accumulate (v)

   a. Over the years, he _____ thousands of books in different languages.

   b. The _____ of knowledge is a never-ending process.

7. distraction (n)   distract (v)   distracted (adj)

   a. Listening to music can be a _____ if you are trying to study at the same time.

   b. I don't think she was listening to me because she had a _____ look on her face.

   c. Every time the telephone rings, it _____ me from my studies.

8. accessibility (n)   accessible (adj)

   a. This building isn't _____ to people in wheelchairs because they can't get up the stairs.

   b. He took a course at Tanana Community College because of its _____; it only takes him ten minutes to get there.

VI.   Sentence Completion

Complete each sentence using the words listed below.

accumulated   forego   pursue   retired   distract   prior   residential

1. At a _____ school, most students live on campus.

2. I have _____ a lot of junk in the past few years; it's time to throw some of it away.

3. I'm going to _____ lunch so that I can eat a big dinner tonight.

4. My brother moved to New York in 1980. _____ to that he lived in San Francisco.

5. It's better if you don't think about your problems now. What can I do to _____ you?

6. Do your parents still work or are they _____?

7. Do you plan to _____ your interest in computers when you go to college?

C O U N T E R P A R T S

1. On the following page are just a few of the many courses listed in the Elderhostel catalog. Read the descriptions and tell which course would be the most interesting to you and why.

2. Many Elderhostel courses relate to the area where the course is offered. For example, Elderhostelers can travel to Arizona to study Arizona Indian culture. Design a new course for the Elderhostel program. Choose a location for your course and write a description of it for the Elderhostel catalog.

3. If you had to design an Elderhostel program for a university near your home town, what three courses would you suggest? What is available in your area that might interest retired Americans? Write a title and description for each course.

4. Some gerontologists—people who study the aging process—say that learning a new language is a good way for older people to keep their minds active and alert. What are some other ways? List your ideas.

5. In 1955, Americans 65 or older made up 8 percent of the population. Today they are 13 percent and soon they might be 20 percent. What effect do you think this change might have? What types of businesses might benefit from this change?

Typical Elderhostel Programs

HOST INSTITUTION: ARIZONA STATE UNIVERSITY, TEMPE, ARIZONA

Frank Lloyd Wright: The Man, The Myth, The Masterworks

A survey of the contribution to modern architecture by the founder of Taliesin, with emphasis on Wrights' structures in the Phoenix area.

Introduction to Arizona/Arizona Indian Culture

Take an arm-chair trip with Marshall Trimble, renowned author-historian, through Arizona's mining and ghost towns and lost treasures. Learn about Arizona Indian cultures.

Enjoyment of Poetry

This course is designed to demonstrate the power and beauty of poetry. The focus of the course will be on enjoyment.

HOST INSTITUTION: CALIFORNIA STATE UNIVERSITY, FRESNO, CALIFORNIA

Volcanoes, Glaciers and Ancient Seas: Geologic History of Central California

Examine the geological history of central California: the volcanic features near Mammoth Lakes, the glacial history of Yosemite, the ancient seas that occupied the San Joaquin Valley, and other areas.

Peru Before the Incas

Several significant civilizations developed in Peru before the Incas. Focus is on such major topics as the origins of agriculture and urbanization and the expansion of political and religious systems.

Jazz Workshop: From Ragtime to Contemporary

Learn to listen to and understand jazz from its European and African roots, through all jazz eras. Recorded and live jazz will be presented.

Globalization and Our Future

Globalization is one of the processes of unifying the diverse peoples of the world. The course contrasts modern globalization trends with imperialism and federalism, concluding with suggestions of optimal solutions.

HOST INSTITUTION: BAYLOR UNIVERSITY, WACO, TEXAS

Skylights: A Brief Encounter with Our Solar System and the Universe

Explore comets, meteors, asteroids, the sun, moon, and the planets of our solar system along with a review of the structure and origin of the universe.

Understanding Our Chemical World

A chemistry professor helps you make sense of chemistry as it affects you from day to day. Polymers, soaps and detergents, cosmetics, food additives, pain killers—what are the benefits and the costs of these things we take for granted?

An Historical Overview of Women and Religion

Find out how women have achieved status in religious institutions throughout history. What are the backgrounds of current issues and concerns about women and their religious roles?

Alone Versus Lonely: An Essay

1. Have you ever felt lonely? What caused you to feel lonely? What happened to make you stop feeling lonely?

2. Do you think it is possible to live alone and not feel lonely? Why or why not?

3. Read the first paragraph of the essay. What is the main idea of this paragraph? Share ideas with your classmates. Then read the rest of the essay and take notes in a chart like this:

Paragraph	Topic or Main Idea
1	
2	
3	
4	
5	

oneliness is not the same as being alone. A person can be just as lonely in a group of people as when home alone. And those who choose solitude° may never be lonely. Rather, loneliness is a feeling of being unconnected with other people, of wanting to be with someone who isn't there, of having no one to turn to who can affirm° one's essential human qualities.

being alone

assure one of

Dr. Robert Weiss, a sociologist at the University of Massachusetts in Boston, has identified two aspects of loneliness: emotional loneliness, marked by an absence of an intimate attachment, such as a love relationship or a marriage; and social loneliness, characterized by the absence of a community or network of friends to whom one feels attached.

According to Dr. Weiss, people need both emotional and social attachments to prevent loneliness; one cannot compensate for the lack of the other. Thus, a happily married woman with small children who is socially isolated is likely to feel lonely because she lacks friends. And someone involved in a bad marriage may not be lonely if the marriage provides a strong connection with another person.

Who is Lonely?

From time to time, loneliness afflicts° nearly everyone. It is usually provoked by a lost connection with significant people in one's life, such as the death of a loved one, going away to college for the first time, or moving away from close friends. This loneliness is usually temporary and decreases with time as one makes new friends and discovers that one can still enjoy life despite the loss.

happens to

But some people are always lonely, and researchers have found that chronic° loneliness comes more from within individuals than it does from circumstances imposed from outside. The studies show that chronically lonely people see themselves and other people quite differently from the way those who are not lonely do. They also have different expectations from relationships, expectations that serve to perpetuate° their loneliness.

habitual

extend, continue

According to Dr. Warren Jones, psychologist at the University of Tulsa, lonely people tend to blame their loneliness on themselves, on their personality and appearance. Thoughts such as "I'm unattractive," "I'm uninteresting," and "I'm worthless," are common themes among the chronically lonely.

In addition, "Lonely people tend not to like the people they meet and assume those people don't like them," Dr. Jones says, in explaining why the lonely have trouble making friends or forming intimate relationships.

Furthermore, many lonely people lack the skills needed to establish meaningful, caring contact with another person. In conversations with potential new friends, the lonely tend to talk more about themselves, to ask fewer questions of the other person, and to change topics° more frequently than a person would who is not lonely, Dr. Jones's studies showed.

subjects

But although some lonely people shy away from° topics that would be self-revealing, others are too quick to reveal intimate facts about themselves, causing new acquaintances to back away, according to Dr. Phillip Shaver, psychologist at the University of Denver. He says, "The lonely tend to be self-focused and self-conscious,° instead of focusing on the other person. You can't start a relationship unless you consider the other person's needs."

shy away from: avoid

overly concerned with oneself

Other studies showed that lonely people know and interact with as many other people as the nonlonely do, but the lonely tend to have unrealistic standards or expectations about relationships that get in the way of forming close friendships. Though searching desperately for relationships to ease their loneliness, they tend to be overly sensitive to any sign of rejection and often back out of relationships because the other person is less than ideally accepting.

Given these characteristics, the data on who is lonely may seem less surprising. Surveys have shown that the loneliest people tend to be adolescents and young adults. Contrary to popular belief, the elderly are less lonely than people in other age groups, perhaps because the elderly have more realistic expectations, reports Dr. Dan Russell, psychologist at the University of Iowa Medical School.

In the young student, Dr. Russell has found, loneliness is commonly tied to the absence of satisfying friendships; in the older student, it is determined by the absence of a romantic relationship. In the elderly, loneliness is linked not to how infrequently they see their children and grandchildren, but to the absence of relationships with peers. Thus, an elderly widow who lives with her daughter's family may be very lonely if she has little contact with friends her own age.

The chances of being lonely are greater if you're poor because you don't have the money to "reach out and touch someone" by phone, or to hire baby-sitters and go out to places where you might meet people you would like.

Studies have shown that the children of divorce are more likely to be lonely as adults, and the younger the child at the time of the divorce, the greater the chances of adult loneliness.

Dr. Jeffrey Young of the University of Pennsylvania has developed a specific therapy° program for very lonely people that starts by focusing on the negative thought processes that perpetuate loneliness. He encourages people to stop blaming themselves for their loneliness. He also encourages them to find a

treatment

solitary activity that they enjoy so they can learn not to fear being alone and instead take pleasure in solitude.

"The problem today is not that relationships are impossible, but that they take more initiative° than they used to," Dr. Shaver said. "Also, people are much more idealistic about what a relationship should provide."

effort to begin

EXERCISES

I.   Comprehension and Discussion Questions

General Ideas
1. Is a person who lives alone necessarily lonely? Explain the difference between loneliness and being alone.

2. What problems do chronically lonely people have in common? How do they feel about themselves? How do they relate to others?

3. According to this article, which age group is the loneliest? Why?

Details
4. This essay includes the ideas of several people. Scan the reading to find their names and ideas and take notes in the chart on the following page.

Name	Profession	Ideas
Dr. Robert Weiss	sociologist	• two kinds of loneliness: emotional and social • people need both emotional and social ties
Dr. Warren Jones		

Opinions

5. What do you think Dr. Russell would advise an elderly widow to do in order to avoid feeling lonely?

6. Do you agree that the chances of feeling lonely are greater if you are poor? Why or why not?

II.   Between the Lines

Choose the answer that completes each of the following statements.

1. The main idea of the first paragraph is that
   a. many people live alone.
   b. being alone and feeling lonely are not the same thing.
   c. lonely people do not feel connected to other people.

2. According to the information in the first paragraph, a person at a party
    a. may feel lonely.
    b. never feels lonely.
    c. always feels lonely.

3. Chronic loneliness is most often caused by
    a. the death of a relative.
    b. moving away from close friends.
    c. an individual's personality problems.

4. In conversations, lonely people often
    a. talk about themselves a lot.
    b. ask other people personal questions.
    c. refuse to talk.

5. A child whose parents divorced when she was _____ is most likely to suffer from loneliness as an adult.
    a. three
    b. nine
    c. fifteen

6. Elderly people are more likely to feel lonely if
    a. they don't live with their children.
    b. they live by themselves.
    c. they don't have people their own age to talk to.

III. Vocabulary in Context

Use context to choose the word or term that best fits the meaning of the italicized words in the sentences below. Circle your answers.

1. Loneliness is not the same as being alone. A person can be just as lonely in a group of people as when home alone. And those who choose solitude may never be lonely. *Rather,* loneliness is a state of feeling unconnected with other people.

    a. In addition   b. Instead   c. For example

2. Dr. Robert Weiss has identified two aspects of loneliness: emotional loneliness, marked by an absence of an *intimate* attachment, such as a love relationship or a marriage; and social loneliness, characterized by the absence of a network of friends.

    a. close   b. happy   c. difficult

3. A happily married woman with small children who is socially *isolated* is likely to feel lonely because she lacks friends.

   a. accepted   b. uncomfortable   c. separated

4. From time to time, loneliness afflicts nearly everyone. It is usually *provoked* by a lost connection with significant people in one's life, such as the death of a loved one.

   a. improved   b. caused   c. discovered

5. Some people are always lonely, and researchers have found that chronic loneliness comes more from within individuals than it does from circumstances *imposed* from outside.

   a. forced on someone   b. enjoyed   c. forgotten

6. Some studies show that lonely people know and interact with as many other people as the nonlonely do, but the lonely tend to have unrealistic standards or expectations about relationships that *get in the way of* forming close friendships.

   a. help in   b. characterize   c. make difficult

7. In the elderly, loneliness is linked not to how infrequently they see their children and grandchildren, but to the *absence* of relationships with peers. Thus, an elderly widow who lives with her daughter's family may be very lonely if she has little contact with friends her own age.

   a. pleasure   b. lack   c. acceptance

IV. Word Forms

Put the correct form of the word in each blank. Check the verb forms for correct tense, number, and voice (active or passive), and check the nouns for number (singular or plural).

1. mobility (n)   mobilization (n)   mobilize (v)   mobile (adj)

   a. If you live in the country without a car, you have no _____.

   b. During the summer the family traveled across the country in their _____ home.

   c. When the war began, the generals ordered the _____ of the troops along the border.

   d. Many organizations across the country are trying to _____ support for the movement against the production of nuclear weapons.

2. provocation (n)   provoke (v)   provocative (adj)

    a. The film was so _____ that we spent hours discussing it after we left the theater.

    b. While he was walking down the street, he was suddenly attacked without

        _____.

    c. The political discussion _____ a fight between two of the students in the class.

3. imposition (n)   impose (v)

    a. He felt that asking her for help would be an _____.

    b. The state government has decided to _____ a higher tax on cigarettes.

4. affliction (n)   afflict (v)

    a. Franklin Delano Roosevelt _____ with polio as a young man.

    b. Despite his _____, he served as president of the United States for four consecutive terms.

5. interaction (n)   interact (v)

    a. The teacher was pleased that the students _____ so well.

    b. The psychologists studied the _____ between the monkey and her newborn baby.

6. solitude (n)   solitary (adj)

    a. The writer, who lived in a cabin in the woods, wrote about the joys of

        _____.

    b. He said that although he led a _____ life, he was never lonely.

7. therapy (n)   therapist (n)   therapeutic (adj)

    a. After several years of _____, she no longer had a fear of heights.

    b. Although he has many emotional problems, he refuses to see a _____.

    c. Studies have shown that this medicine has no _____ value.

8. impersonality (n)   impersonal (adj)

    a. His letter sounded cold and _____.

    b. Many people object to the _____ of computerized banking.

V.   Synonyms

From the list below, choose synonyms for the italicized words and phrases.

theme   characterize   data   chronic   focus on   network   compensated

1. The speaker suggested that we *concentrate our attention on* the problems of unemployment.
2. The *subject* of all his novels is the human struggle against the forces of nature.
3. How would you *describe* your boss?
4. The scientists fed the *information* they had collected into the computer.
5. The doctor told him that his *constant* cough was caused by his heavy smoking.
6. After losing her husband in the accident, she was grateful she could turn to a *close group* of friends for support.
7. The workers complained that they were never *properly paid* for overtime.

COUNTERPARTS

1. Dr. Jeffrey Young encourages lonely people to find a solitary activity that they enjoy so they can learn not to fear being alone. What are some enjoyable solitary activities? List as many things as you can think of. Then compare ideas with a partner.

2. What advice would you give to a student who has just moved to a new country to attend a university? What could this person do to avoid feeling lonely? Make a list of specific suggestions.

3. With a partner, role play a conversation in which a chronically lonely person is talking to a new acquaintance. In your conversation, reveal the characteristics of a chronically lonely person as described by Dr. Jones and Dr. Shaver in the essay.

4. This essay suggests that a person needs to have both close friends and a romantic relationship. Do you agree that both are equally important, or do you feel that one is more important than the other? Do you think that men and women differ in their need for friendship and romantic relationships? Explain your point of view.

It's the Real Thing: People as Art

1. Think of an artist whose work you really like. What do you like about this person's artwork?

2. What does the title of this chapter mean to you? Share ideas with your classmates.

3. The picture on page 75 shows the artist Duane Hanson at work. The picture on page 73 is an example of his work. What information do the pictures give you about this artist and his work? What questions would you like to ask about him? List your ideas and questions in a chart. Then read the article and look for answers to your questions.

Information from the pictures	Questions
He's a sculptor.	*What is he putting on the man's arms?*

CHAPTER 8

Duane Hanson is an unusual artist in a number of ways. He works in the most modern of materials, plastic; but his subject matter is the oldest in art, the human form. Although he has been an artist all of his life, he has only recently become both a critical and a financial success. And he is probably the only artist in America today to say that one of his aims is to reach the non-art loving public and get them to come and look at art. His recent shows have drawn people who say that they have never been to an art gallery or museum before. What attracts them are his amazingly° lifelike figures of ordinary people, some of them doing nothing more extraordinary than sitting in a chair or leaning against a wall.

remarkably

testify to: are proof of

very scared

sleeping lightly

hard building material
accidentally pushed
move

baked clay

make his mark: succeed

one who has fled

dead body
government assistance to poor people

represent
complained about

Many stories testify to° the lifelike quality of the pieces. A thief in an art gallery in Palm Beach, Florida, stumbled into a man in worker's clothes standing in the dark. He turned away, terrified,° to run into the waiting arms of the local police; the worker was a Hanson sculpture. A cleaning lady called the police at Kent State University in Ohio when she failed to awaken Hanson's *Man Dozing° in a Chair.* When the police pulled a gun on him and he remained motionless, she cried, "My God, he's dead!" and fainted.

Even in their museum settings, the plastic figures have been taken for living people. A Wichita, Kansas, journalist describes his meeting with the cement° worker in a torn T-shirt and a hard hat: "As I jostled° him, I said, 'Excuse me.' But he didn't budge,° didn't reply, and I realized he was a Hanson." While the show was at the Portland Art Museum, one viewer, a sculptor in ceramics° himself, commented, "When you go to a museum, you go to look, but at a Hanson show, the sculptures are looking at you. They have the worn quality we accept in real people, and they look like they are here to prepare for the next show."

It took Hanson about thirty years after high school to make his mark° in the art world, but he never wanted to do anything but be a sculptor. After studying and experimenting with several different styles, he began to do sculptures with a social comment. The first one, of a dead Cuban refugee° woman, got a hostile reception from the *Miami Herald*: "This we do not consider a work of art."

Far from discouraged, Hanson went on to produce more figures of social commitment: a corpse° in a box, called *Welfare°-2598?;* a smashed-up motorcycle rider; and Vietnam victims.

Gradually, however, the tone of his work softened as he began to portray° the life that was closer to home. Some critics deplored° what they saw as a return to naturalism, and others complained that Hanson was not serious. Hanson kept sculpting his people, however, at the rate of six or eight a year. After he had won a $500 prize at the Florida state fair, Ivan Karp, owner of the O. K. Harris Gallery in New York, wrote to him, "I think perhaps you're a little too good for the Florida state fair." Hanson decided to move to New York, where he stayed for a couple of years, and Karp told him, "Hanson, I'm going to make you rich and famous." Karp has since represented the artist, who says happily, "He kept his word."

Making a figure is a painstaking° process. First, the model, dressed only in underclothing, is lathered° with mineral oil. Then molds are fashioned for the legs, the arms, the whole torso,° and the head. For the face, somewhat different materials are used. Only the nostrils, mouth, and eyes are left uncovered, so the model can breathe and see. It is not easy to hold the exact pose° Hanson wants with the weight of the mold on the body; and it takes at least two visits by the model to Hanson's studio, and usually three, to get all the molds right.

  When it comes to painting the face, neck, arms, legs, hands, and feet—the part of the job Hanson likes best—he works partly from his memory of the model and partly from his own sense of what will be believable. He puts in blemishes° and variations of skin color that may exaggerate nature, but only slightly. Except for the posing of his subjects, this is the most conventionally "artful" stage of this atypical art, and he spends weeks perfecting the subtleties.°

  When Hanson can't talk a model out of his or her own

with great care
covered

body separate from head and limbs

position

marks

finer details

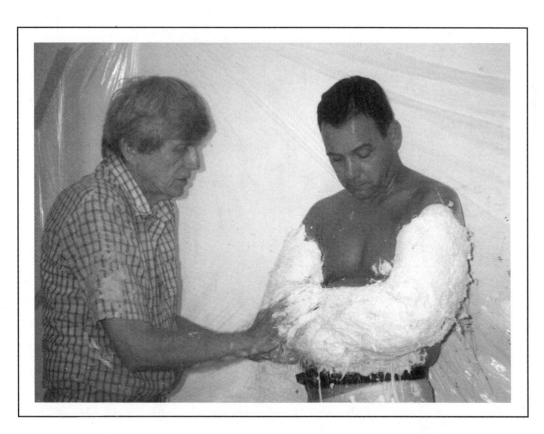

thrift shops: stores selling used objects

collected

head coverings made of hair

put in

carelessly dressed

clothes, he goes to local thrift shops° and buys what he thinks will suit them, hoping for a good fit. He has accumulated° a boxful of old eyeglasses and wristwatches that he likes to try on his figures once they are nearly finished—something like trying clothes on dolls. He no longer uses wigs° on their heads, preferring the more realistic of individually inserted° hairs. In a recent show, there was only one loss reported: the purse was snatched from the floor beside the *Old Woman*—it was empty and originally cost Hanson fifty cents. But he has taken the precaution of screwing down the camera belonging to the old fellow of his *Tourists* couple so it can't be lifted off.

Hanson's feeling for his own work comes out in comments he makes about the individual figures. Of his sloppy° *Super-*

market Shopper, a woman in hair curlers, he says, "She is a symbol of the overconsuming housewife, pushing a cart filled with every imaginable item that she can buy." The older *Lady with Shopping Bags* has been made to seem "a little bigger and heavier to go with the sacks. They help depict° the weighed-down, overconsuming housewife." Asked to sum up his aims, Hanson says, "I think I must be a romantic. I would have liked the eighteenth or nineteenth century, when life was simpler. But we have to deal with the harsh reality of our industrial society. I'm interested in portraying the emptiness, the tragic side of life."

    How collectors look at a Hanson sculpture, as compared with more conventional pieces of art, is a subject that interests Hanson's dealer. Carlo Lamagna, director of the O. K. Harris Gallery, says, "Part of having a Hanson is its shock value." He sees the works as being "about anguish"° and believes an owner needs a big space to contain one, "so you can get away from it.

describe visually

pain

individual judgment

change, exaggeration

special order

It's not the kind of thing you want to have in a small apartment."A New York lawyer who owns the Hanson *Rock Singer* keeps the work in his office."There's nothing more mysterious than the real person," this owner says. The merit of Hanson's work, he feels, is that, "There is no interpretation,° no distortion.° It is the man without his shadow."

So far, Hanson has not accepted any commission° for a portrait because choosing his own models is the way he comments on the life around him. He has done his own father, though, and even himself—although he's not entirely satisfied with the piece. "It is a bit like listening to your own voice on a tape

make a mold of

recorder," he says. One of these days he plans to cast° himself again.

Hanson has considered using a different kind of mold that could produce several copies of any figure. But he wants to continue making only one of each. That is the way he sees the world: a collection of distinct individuals about whom he wants to say something. "It is a wild and wonderful world," he says, "and the most interesting part is the people. They have their problems, their beauty, and their black side, too. It's a tremen-

confront people with: make them look at

dous challenge. . . to confront people with° themselves."

EXERCISES

I.   Comprehension and Discussion Questions

General Ideas
1.   What is special or unusual about Duane Hanson's work?

2.   How has Hanson's work changed over the years?

3.   What are Hanson's aims as an artist?

Details
4.   Describe a Hanson figure. What does it look like? What is it made of?

5.   How is a Hanson figure created? Describe the process.

Opinions
6.   Hanson says that he never wanted to do anything but be a sculptor. What does this tell you about Hanson?

7. Do you think Hanson's sculptures are works of art? Why or why not?

8. Would you model for Duane Hanson? Why or why not?

II. Between the Lines

Choose the answer that completes each of the following statements.

1. The main idea of the second paragraph is that
   a. Hanson's figures look like real people.
   b. people often think Hanson's figures are real.
   c. Hanson's figures can frighten people.

2. How did Hanson's early work differ from his recent work?
   a. His early figures were not ordinary people.
   b. He was more critical of his figures.
   c. His figures have become less realistic.

3. One of his earliest pieces, entitled *Welfare-2598?*, depicted a corpse in a box. What statement do you think he is making in this piece?
   a. Poor people are just numbers.
   b. More people should collect welfare.
   c. The welfare system helps many poor people.
   Can you offer any other interpretation?

4. Hanson is considered an unusual artist because
   a. he works in plastic.
   b. his subject matter is the human form.
   c. he is popular with the general public.

5. Explain the "shock value" of Hanson's work.
   a. It shows people with problems.
   b. His sculptures look like real people.
   c. His figures are frightening.

6. In the 10th paragraph Hanson says that he must be a "romantic." He means that
   a. he loves his art.
   b. he is always in love.
   c. he is attracted to an earlier age.

7. Reread Hanson's comments about his work. Then decide which of the following statements he would probably *disagree* with.

    a. The purpose of art is to depict life as it should be.

    b. It is shocking for people to see themselves as they are.

    c. Life is more complicated now than it was in the past.

III.   Sentence Completion

Put the correct word in each blank. Choose from the words listed below.

depicts   distortion   lathering   pose   plastic   confront

sculptor   model   sculpture   lifelike   mold   style

Duane Hanson is a(n) _____ who works in _____.
He creates figures that are so _____ that people sometimes believe they are
alive. Creating a piece of _____ is a long and difficult process. First, Hanson
must find a _____ to _____ for him. Then, after
_____ the model with mineral oil, he creates the _____,
which he then paints and dresses. Hanson _____ people as they are with a
minimum of _____. This _____ is called naturalism. Hanson's
work attracts people who don't often go to art galleries or museums. They are fascinated by the
figures that resemble themselves and people they know. This, Hanson says, is his purpose—"to
_____ people with themselves."

IV.   Vocabulary in Context

Use context to choose the word or term that best fits the meaning of the italicized words in the sentences below. Circle your choices.

1. Hanson is probably the only artist in America today to say that one of his aims is to reach the non-art public and get them to come and look at art. His recent shows have *drawn* people who say that they have never been to an art gallery or museum before.

    a. bored   b. angered   c. attracted

2. A cleaning lady called the police at Kent State University in Ohio when she failed to awaken Hanson's "Man Dozing in a Chair." When the police *pulled a gun on* him and he remained motionless, she cried, "My God, he's dead!" and fainted.

    a. pointed a gun at   b. shot at   c. took a gun from

3. Even in museum settings, the plastic figures have been *taken for* living people. A Wichita, Kansas journalist describes his meeting with the sculpture of a cement worker in a torn T-shirt and a hard hat: "As I jostled him, I said, 'Excuse me.' But he didn't budge, didn't reply, and I realized he was a Hanson."

   a. stolen by   b. thought to be   c. looked at by

4. After studying and experimenting with several different styles, Hanson began to do sculptures with a social comment. The first one, of a dead Cuban refugee, got a *hostile* reception from the Miami Herald: "This we do not consider a work of art."

   a. unfriendly   b. lengthy   c. good

5. Hanson decided to move to New York, where he stayed for a couple of years. Gallery owner Ivan Karp told him, "Hanson, I'm going to make you rich and famous." Karp has since represented the artist, who says happily, "He *kept his word.*"

   a. repeated himself   b. didn't say anything   c. did as he promised

6. A New York lawyer who owns the Hanson "Rock Singer" keeps the work in his office. "There's nothing more mysterious than the real person," this owner says. The merit of Hanson's work, he feels, is that, "There is no interpretation, no distortion. *It* is the man without his shadow."

   It refers to

   a. the merit.   b. Hanson's work.   c. the real person.

7. So far, Hanson has not accepted any commissions for a portrait because choosing his own models is the way he comments on the life around him. He has done his own father, though, and even himself—though he's not entirely satisfied with *the piece.*

   The piece refers to

   a. Hanson's sculpture of himself.

   b. Hanson's sculpture of his father.

   c. Hanson's sculpture of his model.

V.   Word Forms

Put the correct form of the word in each blank. Check the verb forms for correct tense, number, and voice (active or passive), and check the nouns for number (singular or plural).

1. journal (n)   journalist (n)   journalism (n)

   a. The results of her research were recently reported in the *New England* _____ *of Medicine.*

   b. The _____ was killed while covering a story in Southeast Asia.

   c. The Pulitzer Prize-winning writer had attended Columbia's School of

      _____.

2. portray (v)   portrayal (n)   portrait (n)

    a. Hanson's sculpture _____ ordinary people.

    b. In a famous novel by Oscar Wilde, the main character's _____ ages while he himself remains youthful.

    c. The actor's sensitive _____ of a Vietnam veteran won him an Academy Award.

3. subtlety (n)   subtle (adj)   subtly (adv)

    a. She _____ changed the topic of conversation to avoid discussing the issue.

    b. The critics praised the authors' style for its _____ and precision.

    c. The meaning of the poem was so _____ that it required several readings.

4. variety (n)   variation (n)   vary (v)   various (adj)   variable (adj)

    a. The series of paintings were _____ on the same theme.

    b. Fall weather is quite _____ in the Northeast.

    c. The sweater is available in a _____ of colors.

    d. The taste of tap water _____ in different parts of the country.

    e. He had _____ complaints about the company and its business practices.

5. interpreter (n)   interpretation (n)   interpret (v)

    a. After working for several years as an _____ at the United Nations, she obtained a position at the American Embassy in Athens.

    b. I don't agree with your _____ of the ending of the story.

    c. Her reply was puzzling, he didn't know how to _____ it.

6. hostility (n)   hostile (adj)

    a. When asked about his former life, he suddenly became cold and _____.

    b. He couldn't understand the reason for her _____ toward him.

7. amazement (n)   amaze (v)   amazed (adj)   amazing (adj)

    a. The monkey's trick _____ the audience.

    b. As a result of his _____ resemblance to the real criminal, he was falsely accused of committing the crime.

    c. I was _____ at how much the child had grown since my last visit.

    d. He was shocked by my answer and stared at me in _____.

VI. Synonyms

From the list below, choose synonyms for the italicized words and phrases.

corpse   deplored   confronted   dozing   painstakingly   terrified   stumbled   budge

1. The police demanded that he get up, but he refused to *move*.
2. Two children discovered the *dead body* in the woods behind their home.
3. When *faced* with the truth about what really happened, he refused to believe it.
4. They *very carefully* removed the bomb from the box it had been sent in.
5. The drunk *tripped* and fell as he was leaving the bar.
6. When we entered the room, we found her *sleeping* on the sofa with a book in her lap.
7. *Very frightened* by the strange noises they heard in the middle of the night, the couple called the police.
8. She *strongly disapproved of* his behavior at the party.

C O U N T E R P A R T S

1. Duane Hanson is a popular American artist; his work interests people who don't normally go to art galleries or museums. His success is due, in part, to the fact that his subject matter is real people. Think of an artist who is popular in your country. What is his or her medium (painting, sculpture, photography)? What is his or her subject matter? Describe some of his or her famous works and tell why you think this artist is popular.

2. When an artist has an exhibit, the museum or art gallery where the work is being shown often distributes a "publicity release." This is a brief description of the artist's life and work written in a lively style designed to attract people to the exhibit. Using the information in the article, write a "publicity release" for Duane Hanson.

3. Much has been said about the realism of Hanson's figures; they depict ordinary people in everyday situations. Yet, in the article, Hanson and some of his collectors have noted that in some ways his figures are not realistic. Consider their comments and study the picture of the Hanson piece on page 73. Tell how you think Hanson's figures resemble real people and how they do not.

1. You can read your daily horoscope in many newspapers in the United States. The horoscope below is for people born between August 23rd and September 22nd.

> **Virgo (Aug. 23–Sept. 22)**
>
> *You are very strong today. Even though you might run into some disagreement, don't worry about it. Shop for something beautiful if you have the money.*

Why do you think people read their daily horoscopes?

2. Read the introduction on page 85. Do you think horoscopes provide useful information? Why or why not?

3. As you read the following article, take notes in a chart like the one below. Add the signs of the zodiac and the characteristics of people born under each sign.

Sign of the Zodiac	Birth Dates	Characteristics of people with this sign
Aries	March 21–April 19	jealous, impatient
Taurus		

The head of an advertising agency in San Francisco claims that she doesn't make any business decisions for the day until she reads her horoscope° in the morning newspaper. She is one of more than forty million Americans who believe that astrology° can predict° whether the day will be favorable— or unfavorable—for business, friendship, or even love. In addition to general daily advice, horoscopes are consulted for specific purposes. If you want to know what kind of luck you may have in romance, you can find out by reading this article, which specialized in love. Skeptical?° Then find your sign below, and then decide how well it describes you—and the one(s) you love.

information based on stars

study of how stars affect our lives/tell in advance

doubtful

The Zodiac and Love

Aries—March 21 to April 19

The first sign of the zodiac is Aries. If you were born between March 21 and April 19, you are under the influence of Aries and its ruling planet, Mars. Mars is a very fiery planet and gives you energy in every way. It is therefore quite natural that love affairs play a great part in your life. Sometimes you don't know where to stop. When one love affair comes to an end, you take only a little time to recover before you are off on another emotional adventure. Unfortunately, you are often jealous and impatient.° You can rarely have a love affair without stormy times between you and your partner. However, you are also forgiving and always willing to forget, even though your partner might not be. Relationships can be difficult for members of this sign— but remember, they will also never be dull. Perhaps the most harmonious° sign for Aries as a life partner is Libra: Libras possess qualities that many Aries lack: kindness, tolerance,° and sympathy. In certain circumstances, Gemini and Sagittarians can be compatible with Aries.

unable to wait

agreeable, not conflicting
acceptance of others

worthy of notice

unwilling

work hard

able to exist comfortably

Taurus—April 20 to May 20

If you were born between April 20 and May 20, you are under the influence of the sign of Taurus. One of the most notable° characteristics of a Taurus is possessiveness, not only in relation to material things, but in attitudes toward love. Taurians consider change quite difficult and are reluctant° to adapt to new situations. Because Taurians are under the influence of the beauty-loving planet Venus, they enjoy the company of the opposite sex because of their sensitivity to physical beauty. Taurians are motivated by the thought of marriage, children, a gracious home, and enough money to show off their possessions. In addition, they want tremendous appreciation from their mates. But Taurians are very loving partners and strive° to be happy in their relationships. They are capable of fulfilling their obligations and make committed marriage partners. Scorpio, Virgo, and Libra are quite compatible° with Taurus.

moving quickly

cope with: manage

Gemini—May 21 to June 21

If you were born between May 21 and June 21, you are under the influence of Gemini. This is one of the most complicated signs in the zodiac, especially when it comes to love. The symbol for the Gemini is twins, which indicates a dual nature. Often, Geminis feel pulled in opposite directions in their love lives. Even at an early age, Geminis can have strong and meaningful love affairs and tend to fall in love easily. In fact, it seems as though Geminis are always in love. As a result, they have the reputation of being the "butterflies" of the zodiac, flitting° from one relationship to another. Although Geminis seek to be in love, they often cannot cope with° the responsibilities involved; therefore, they need a great deal of understanding from their partners. It is not easy to generalize about this complex sign, but Aries, Leos, Libras, and Sagittarians come the closest to being compatible with Geminis.

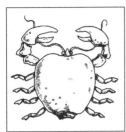

ray of moonlight

Cancer—June 22 to July 22

If you were born between June 22 and July 22, you are under the influence of the sign Cancer. This is probably one of the most interesting signs of the zodiac, for within its orbit lie all the major influences on the emotions. Cancers of both sexes tend to be highly emotional. Trying to understand the Cancer female is rather like trying to catch a moonbeam.° More than any other sign, the Cancer woman wants to be courted,° spoiled, and pampered.° She is also sensitive to all things concerning her family and has a deep love for the comforts of her home. The Cancer man is peaceful enough if allowed to have his own way but is able to inflict° harm if provoked.° Extremely understanding, he easily comprehends° a woman's nature and will share in household tasks and child raising. Yet, the Cancer male himself needs a lot of understanding to retain his dignity and balance in life. The ideal relationship for a Cancer is with other Cancers, or with a Scorpio or a Pisces.

sought after
spoiled and pampered: treated too well

cause/angered
understands

Leo—July 23 to August 22

If you were born between July 23 and August 22, you are under the influence of Leo. People born under this sign are known to be extremely loyal, but most of all, Leos are known to be great lovers, especially the male Leos. However, they must find someone who can light their fire and keep it going. They like to be married, but even then they have a reputation for a roving eye.° Leo men can be domineering and like to rule the household. This is also true of Leo women, so that marriage between two Leos is not a very good idea. Women born under this sign have a strong sense of family and duty. They want to be good wives and mothers but not at the expense of sacrificing their own interests. Many Leo women handle careers and family life well together. Compatible signs for Leos are Aquarius, Aries, and Libra.

roving eye: interest in other partners

Virgo—August 23 to September 22

If you were born between August 23 and September 22, you are under the influence of Virgo. Although this is known as the sign of service, this does not seem to apply to Virgos' love lives. In fact, Virgos are thought to be rather arrogant,° perhaps because of their tendency to analyze° and criticize the person they are likely to fall in love with. Virgos are discriminating° in their choices and, once they have chosen a partner, feel satisfied. They seek, more than any other sign of the zodiac, intellectual companionship; other romantic considerations are secondary. Virgos are totally sincere, and when a Virgo says, "I love you," you can believe it. (Once Virgos are married, they become the most considerate of mates.) A Virgo of either sex can find a satisfying relationship with a Taurian, a Capricorn, or even another Virgo.

overly proud
study in detail

careful

connecting

opposed/
removed

harm

Libra—September 23 to October 23

If you were born between September 23 and October 23, you are under the influence of Libra. Libra is a bridge, the linking° sign between the emotional coolness of Virgo and the contrasting passion of Scorpio. In a sign joining these two extremes, it is natural to find characteristics that are complicated, and even contradictory.° Libras are known to be remote,° yet they seem to need marriage more than any other sign of the zodiac. Most Librans tend toward early marriage but do not stay with the same person for a lifetime. They are also known for their desire for perfection, which can often be to their detriment.° Not able to settle for someone less than perfect, they can make themselves miserable trying to find someone flawless. A love affair with a Libra, if you can get through the first two years, stands a chance of being stable because a Libran's strongest desire is for harmony. The most compatible signs for Libras are Aries, Leo, and Sagittarius.

disturbed

open, flowing

characteristic

giving in to
end

Scorpio—October 24 to November 21

If you were born between October 24 and November 21, you are under the influence of Scorpio, one of the strongest and most intense signs. Because Scorpio is a water sign, a Scorpio's character is often turbulent.° As we know, water can boil and change into steam, but it always retains its original nature of being fluid° and free. Because of this independence, Scorpios rarely allow another person to get close to them. They don't like to reveal their innermost thoughts, and this trait° makes it difficult to understand Scorpios and to start a romantic relationship with them. They are often more concerned with sex than with love, and this tendency can get both the male and the female into trouble. There is nothing delicate, sweet, or submissive° about a Scorpio woman. When she feels that it is time to terminate° a relationship, she does it quickly. No one is more capable of destroying a romance, often at the height of its beauty, than the Scorpio. Because this sign has so many individual traits within it, it is hard to recommend compatible signs, although other water signs—Pisces and Cancer—seem to attract the Scorpio; Taurus can also be a candidate.

Sagittarius—November 22 to December 21

If you were born between November 22 and December 21, you are under the influence of the sign Sagittarius, ruled by the planet Jupiter. This planet is known to be quite benevolent. Many of the generous qualities of Jupiter are reflected in the Sagittarian nature. Sagittarians are easygoing, have attractive manners, and love to offer friendship to anyone who will accept it. This trait can be disastrous° because they sometimes mistake friendship for love. The value they place on being liked gives them the reputation for being flirts.° But Sagittarians think of the opposite sex in terms of companionship first and romance second. Marriages with members of this sign can offer a steady and stable life because they are often old-fashioned in their ideas of love. In fact, marriage to a Sagittarian will never be lonely because the Sagittarian is a genius at making friends. His or her home is likely to be filled with people of all ages as well as numerous pets. Sagittarians find the most satisfactory lives, from a romantic point of view, with Geminis. A Leo or a Libra can also be a good partner.

very bad luck

make-believe lovers

Capricorn—December 22 to January 19

If you were born between December 22 and January 19, you are under the influence of Capricorn. It is not unusual for Capricorns to have difficulties in their love lives, partly because they often make the same mistake more than once. They tend to fall in love with the same kind of person over and over again, even if that sort of person is not good for them. It can take a long time for them to break out of this tragic romantic cycle.° The Capricorn male and female are quite different in their romantic attitudes. The Capricorn male is a lawmaker by instinct. He wants others to obey him and can be unforgiving and harsh.° The female, on the other hand, can be almost a saint. She is very giving and willing to make great sacrifices for her beloved. Capricorn men seem most happy with Pisces or Scorpio women; female Capricorns do best with Cancer males.

complete circle of events

rough, unpleasant

natural, inborn

Aquarius—January 20 to February 18

If you were born between January 20 and February 18, then you are under the sign of Aquarius. This is one of the signs in the zodiac where there is not a great deal of difference between the male and female attitudes toward sex and romance. Aquarians have a tremendous capacity to love and can even love more than one person at a time. This trait does not mean that they are unfaithful, but simply philosophical: they see love as a life force and feel that there is enough to go around. When they do choose to get married or to live with someone, they are totally committed. The search for a permanent relationship is easier for them because they have an intuitive° sense of what is good for them. Aries, Leo, and Gemini are suitable combinations for Aquarius.

very sociable/not very sociable

controlling

Pisces—February 19 to March 20

If you were born between February 19 and March 20, you are under the influence of Pisces. This is the twelfth sign of the zodiac. It is symbolized by two fishes swimming in different directions, which gives some indication of the complications of the lives of Pisceans, especially their love lives. Pisceans are so complicated and diverse in character that it is difficult to understand them when it comes to romance. Pisceans may be either extroverts° or introverts;° they may pursue or may like being pursued. They also have a difficult time making up their minds in affairs of the heart. They need strong partners to guide them but will back away if the partner is too domineering.°

Pisces do not have an easy time finding compatible mates, but they can be very good with other water signs, such as Scorpios.

The Zodiac and License Plates

In the province of Ontario, Canada, they have found a new use of the signs of the zodiac: license plate reading. It all began when the department of motor vehicles° required that each driver's birth month be displayed° on the license plate of his or her car. The idea was to facilitate° yearly driver's license renewal. But astrologer Sheila Kendall soon found that there was a connection between the sign you were born under and the kind of driver you might be, and even what kind of car you might prefer. When a number of Canadian drivers were interviewed on a television news show, they found Miss Kendall's observations surprisingly accurate.° Do you?

cars, truck, etc.
shown
make easier

exact

Aries people are fast, the sportscar types, very energetic drivers.

Taurians are quite different. They're slow, the Sunday drivers, as they're often called.

Geminis come next. They're the little peppy° ones that rush all over the place, weave° through traffic, and are able to park anywhere.

Cancer should be easily identified. They have something personalized dangling° in the window. The Cancer's car would be a home.

Leos are the grand people and they like impressive cars. They drive right up to the door, get out rather grandly, and expect someone else to park their car.

Virgos have practical cars. They might even have a little truck.

Libras, the beautiful people, have beautiful cars. They probably have more than one person in the car because Libras like companions always.

Scorpios probably have powerful cars—with tinted° windows because they like privacy. They could even be bulletproof.°

Sagittarians would probably like sunshine roofs, or convertibles.° They would also have ski racks because they're sporty people.

Capricorns have much more sedate cars, perhaps brown or executive black—very sensible cars, but good powerful ones.

Aquarians might have any sort of car, but it would probably be full of people. They might have an aerial° sticking up because they like to communicate.

Pisces are likely to have blue, green, or gray cars—their colors. They are perhaps a little confused as drivers and may drive around the block once or twice. They're not quite sure where they're going.

The interviewer, Judy Darling, made these final observations. There are two dangers inherent in° this new form of astrological forecasting.° First, most of the signs span° more than one month, so you can't be absolutely sure you have the true sign. Second, by the time you're close enough to read the months on the license plates, you're too close!

Glossary (margin):

- peppy° — full of energy
- weave° — move in and out
- dangling° — hanging
- tinted° — lightly colored
- bullet-proof.° — capable of resisting gunshots
- convertibles.° — cars with removable tops
- aerial° — metal rod for receiving broadcasts
- inherent in° — part of
- forecasting.° — predicting/bridge
- span° — predicting/bridge

EXERCISES

I. Matching Exercise

Below are brief descriptions of eleven of the signs. Match the correct sign to each description. Then go back to the article to check your answers.

Gemini	Aquarius	Sagittarius	Libra
Aries	Taurus	Capricorn	Virgo
Scorpio	Leo	Cancer	

_____ 1. Great lovers; very loyal; domineering; both male and female want to run the house.

_____ 2. Possessive of both material things and people; find change difficult.

_____ 3. Sincere; seek intellectual companionship; very careful in choosing a partner.

_____ 4. Male is a lawmaker; female is very forgiving; both repeat the same mistakes in love.

_____ 5. Very energetic; often jealous and impatient.

_____ 6. Highly emotional; home and family are very important; should seek a partner who is also a water sign.

_____ 7. Intense; strong; very independent; difficult to get close to.

_____ 8. Kind; generous; very sociable; make steady and stable marriage partners.

_____ 9. Seek perfection in partners; have complicated, sometimes contradictory characteristics.

_____ 10. Fall in love easily; often feel pulled in opposite directions.

_____ 11. Can love more than one person at the same time; make committed marriage partners.

II.   Vocabulary in Context

Use context to guess the meaning of the italicized words below. Then look up each word in a dictionary. Choose the definition that best fits the meaning of the word in this context.

1.   When one love affair comes to an end, you take only a little time to *recover* before you are off on another emotional adventure.

      My guess: _____

      Dictionary definition: _____

2.   Libras possess qualities that many Aries *lack*: kindness, tolerance, and sympathy.

      My guess: _____

      Dictionary definition: _____

3.   The symbol for the Gemini is twins, which indicates a *dual* nature. Often, Geminis feel pulled in opposite directions in their love lives.

      My guess: _____

      Dictionary definition: _____

4.   Virgos are totally *sincere,* and when a Virgo says, "I love you," you can believe it.

      My guess: _____

      Dictionary definition: _____

5.   Libra is a bridge, the *linking* sign between the emotional coolness of Virgo and the contrasting passion of Scorpio.

      My guess: _____

      Dictionary definition: _____

6.   Not able to settle for someone less than perfect, Libras can make themselves miserable trying to find someone *flawless.*

      My guess: _____

      Dictionary definition: _____

7.   The planet Jupiter is known to be quite *benevolent.* Many of the generous qualities of Jupiter are reflected in the Sagittarian nature.

      My guess: _____

      Dictionary definition: _____

III. Word Forms

Put the correct form of the word in each blank. Check the verb forms for correct tense, number, and voice (active or passive), and check the nouns for number (singular or plural).

1. prediction (n)   predict (v)   predictable (adj)

    a. The president _____ that the economy will improve this year.

    b. All of the fortune-teller's _____ came true.

    c. The results of the election are _____; everyone knows who is going to win.

2. tolerance (n)   tolerate (v)   tolerant (adj)

    a. I cannot _____ smoking in elevators.

    b. She was always _____ of her son's misbehavior.

    c. The teacher had no _____ for anyone who disagreed with her.

3. termination (n)   terminate (v)   terminal (adj)

    a. The doctors told her that she had _____ cancer.

    b. After the incident, the two countries _____ their trade agreement.

    c. The _____ of the contract was agreed upon by both sides.

4. motivation (n)   motive (n)   motivate (v)   motivated (adj)

    a. To master a foreign language as an adult you must be very _____.

    b. He never succeeded in the business world because he lacked _____.

    c. She tried to _____ her son to do more work at school.

    d. The police asked him his _____ for committing the crime.

5. comprehension (n)   comprehend (v)   comprehensible (adj)

    a. He could speak well, but his reading _____ was poor.

    b. We had to rewrite the report to make it more _____.

    c. She could not _____ the seriousness of her crime.

6. loyalty (n)   loyal (adj)   loyally (adv)

    a. It was difficult to understand his _____ to a country that had kept him in prison for ten years.

    b. Although he lived in the United States for many years, he remained _____ to his native country.

    c. Whenever anyone criticized his country, he would _____ defend it.

7. analysis (n)   analyze (v)   analytical (adj)

   a. To be a good scientist, you need to have an _____ mind.

   b. If you _____ the problem carefully, I'm sure you'll come up with a solution.

   c. After a careful _____ of the situation, we decided on a course of action.

IV. Antonyms

In each of the following groups of words, circle the two that are opposite in meaning.

1. pampered   forgiving   impatient   unspoiled

2. water   steam   fluid   solid

3. fiery   submissive   domineering   benevolent

4. introvert   skeptic   genius   extrovert

5. turbulent   calm   unforgiving   generous

6. peppy   motivated   eager   reluctant

7. obey   terminate   strive   begin

8. harsh   gentle   compatible   friendly

COUNTERPARTS

1. Astrology exists in different forms all over the world. Is the system described in this article similar to the one found in your native country? Is astrology popular in your native country? Do newspapers print horoscopes? Report your answers to the class and together make a class chart on the board.

Country	Similar system?	Popular?	Horoscopes in newspapers?

What conclusions can you draw from the information in your chart?

2. Reread the information about your sign. Make a chart listing the characteristics of people with your sign. Then tell if these characteristics describe you.

Characteristics of my Sign	Describes me	Doesn't describe me
is rather arrogant		✔
seeks intellectual companionship	✔	
discriminating in the choice of a partner	✔	
is sincere	✔	

Based on your chart, do you think horoscopes provide accurate information?

3. Astrologer Sheila Kendall thinks there is a connection between the sign you were born under and the type of car you might prefer. Follow the steps below to test her idea.

a. At the top of an index card, write your astrological sign.

b. On the same index card, briefly describe a car you like.

c. Interview two or three people outside of class. Find out their dates of birth and ask them to describe their favorite cars. Make an index card for each of these people.

d. Put your cards together with your classmates' cards. Then group the cards by astrological sign.

e. Read the cards for each sign to see if there are any similarities. Do people of the same sign prefer the same type of car?

f. Based on your experiment, do you agree or disagree with Sheila Kendall?

The Chili Cookoff: Some Like It Hot

1. Think of a popular dish in your native country. What is it made of? When do people eat it? Tell a partner about this dish.

2. A cookoff is a cooking contest. Study the pictures in this chapter. What information do the pictures give you about chili cookoffs? List your ideas.

3. Think of three things you would like to find out about a chili cookoff. Write your ideas as questions. Then read the article and look for answers to your questions.

In Texas, they take chili seriously. So seriously that from May to November, hundreds of Texans devote their weekends to cooking giant pots of it in chili cookoffs. These contests are carefully organized in cities and towns throughout the state, each one boasting that it sponsors the best one around. Even though other states have their own version° of the cookoff, Texas sets the standards. The Chili Appreciation Society International in Dallas has established rules and regulations° as well as a point system° for determining the winners. There is even a newspaper, the *Goat Gap Gazette* in Houston, that is exclusively° for chili heads, the name given to those devoted to chili making. It publishes a complete list of competitions in the United States and provides useful hints and bits of gossip° for its subscribers.°

The actual cooking for the competition is done in teams, which sport colorful names such as Too Hot to Stop and the Cross-Eyed° Mule Team. The general requirement is that each group must cook from scratch, meaning no precooked or preprepared ingredients. Although the teams are serious about winning (first prize is usually a trophy° but is sometimes cash), they are equally intent on having a good time doing it. All contests are accompanied by a variety of entertainment, from bands to beauty contests to balloon° rides—and a good dose° of drinking, dancing, and visiting.

For some, the local competition is primarily a way to qualify for the event for the true aficionado:° the World Championship Chili Cookoff. In this contest, hometown winners come to compete against each other for prizes that can add up to thousands of dollars. When the championship was first held in 1967, in the little town of Terlingua, Texas, it attracted five hundred people. It grew steadily each year until, in 1982, eight thousand people showed up. No one was more surprised than Frank Tolbert, one of the founders of the original contest. "We didn't realize that we were creating an international subculture," he commented recently, especially as the first championship was intended as a humorous way to promote *A Bowl of Red,* Tolberts' book on chili and other native foods.

The first cookoff was between only two people: Beverly Hills restaurant owner Daven Chasen, who claimed his chili

type

detailed rules/**point system:** method of keeping score

only

informal news/one who receives something regularly

when eyes look at nose

object given as an award

large bag filled with hot air/amount

fan

was the best in the land, and New York writer H. Allen Smith. The latter had written a magazine article entitled "Nobody Knows More About Chili Than I Do." Smith claimed that (1) Texans couldn't cook chili and (2) Smith could. The judging took place on the front porch of the mining-town company store in Terlingua. The judges were blindfolded° while they tasted the chili; the contest ended in a draw.°

had their eyes covered
equal scores

Since then, thousands have made the journey to Terlingua, some to compete and be judged, others just for the fun of watching the spectacle° and eating their fill. In recent years, the enormous turnout has presented more than a few prob-

big show

lems for the little ghost town.° Sometimes chili heads can be a
rowdy° bunch, perhaps partly because of the large quantity of
beer that is consumed while making and tasting the spicy° pots
of chili. After the last cookoff, the town of Terlingua decided to
remodel° the local jail,° just in case it would be needed. Next
time, they expect that as many as ten thousand people will
arrive for the annual championship weekend of November 29,
all in search of that perfect "bowl of red."

The origin of chili is a subject of hot debate among chili
historians. The word *chili* in Spanish means "pepper." But chili
does not seem to have originated in Mexico, as many people
assume. It has been suggested that it all began when travelers
to the West brought dried beef and peppers with them to stew°
with water and eat on the trail. Others think that Texans invented chili to make the then-tough beef more tasty. But, whatever its origins, visitors to Texas in the late 1800s observed it
being cooked over open fires in the plazas° of San Antonio.
Since then it has become a staple° Texas food, and in 1977, it
was named the official Texas dish.

Texans believe that the only real chili is Texas chili. "East-
erners," it is said in Dallas, "clearly have no understanding of
the stuff." And they don't think that Californians do either:
"They put funny kinds of things in their chili … green peppers
… celery." "Genuine Texas chili," states cookbook author Frank
Tolbert and founder of the World Championship Chili Cookoff,
"is just chili peppers and meat," and, he adds, the spices° cumin

ghost town: deserted town
rough, loud

hot in taste, peppery

partly rebuild/prison

cook by boiling slowly

public squares
basic

foods that flavor

improve
addition
professional cooks

cooking directions

and a little oregano to enhance° the flavor. No tomatoes. No onion. No beans. Except as a garnish° before serving. But that doesn't seem to prevent other chili chefs° from putting everything in the pot—from whole rabbits to bottles of beer.

Listed on the next two pages are two recipes° that you might run across in a Texas chili competition, along with some helpful hints on how to get the best results.

These recipes are from a pamphlet entitled "Confessions of a Texas Chili Cookoff Champ" by Peter Dossing.

4 lbs. chili meat (round steak or chuck)

Brown in a heavy iron pot with the following until light-colored:

1 large onion, chopped
2 cloves garlic, finely chopped

Add the following:

1 tsp. ground oregano
1 tsp. cumin (comino) seed
6 tsp. chili powder (more if needed)
2 cans tomatoes with green chilies
Salt to taste
2 cups hot water

Bring to a boil, lower heat, and simmer about one hour. Skim off fat during cooking.

This was always a favorite around the house, simple to make and easy to eat. The local newspaper would print this in their food section at least once a week in response to reader requests . . . a very popular recipe.

6 lbs. beef chuck steak, cubed

Brown in a big pot with grease:

  2 large onions, chopped fine
  1 bell pepper, chopped fine
  3 cloves fresh garlic, chopped fine

When onions are transparent, throw 2 lbs. of meat into pot to draw in full flavor. Salt and pepper to taste. Add rest of meat to brown after basic meat has browned.

After browning, add half of the following spices (save rest until a a half hour before judging):

  1 Tbsp. salt
  1 Tbsp. black pepper, crushed type, not ground
  1 Tbsp. Accent
  3 Tbsp. cumin
  8 Tbsp. chili powder
  1 Tbsp. paprika
  1 Tbsp. ground oregano
  1/2 tsp. ground celery seed

Also add:

  1 can spicy tomatoes, chopped up
  1 8-oz. can tomato sauce
Cook for 1 1/2 hours.

DON'T FORGET THE CHILI POT!!
A good pot can make a big difference in your chili. If it cooks evenly, it will just naturally taste better. Iron pots work best, but a new pot must be well-prepared or the iron will alter° the taste of the chili.

change

E X E R C I S E S

I.   Comprehension and Discussion Questions

General Ideas
1.   What is the purpose of a chili cookoff?
2.   What role did Frank Tolbert play in the first World Championship Chili Cookoff?
3.   How has the World Championship Chili Cookoff changed over the years?

Details
4.   Scan the reading to find answers to these questions:

 a.   Where are chili cookoffs popular?

 b.   Where and when did the first World Championship Chili Cookoff take place?

 c.   What activities, in addition to the chili making competition, take place at chili cookoffs?

 d.   Where did chili come from?

Opinions
5.   Why do so many people attend chili cookoffs?
6.   Would you like to attend the World Championship Chili Cookoff? Why or why not?
7.   If you lived in Terlingua, Texas, how would you feel about the World Championship Chili Cookoff? Why?

II.   Vocabulary in Context

Use context to choose the word or term that best fits the meaning of the italicized words in the sentences below. Circle your answer.

1.   Although the teams are serious about winning (first prize is usually a trophy but sometimes is cash), they are equally *intent on* having a good time doing it.

 a.   sorry about   b.   serious about   c.   discouraged from

2.   Chili cookoffs are carefully organized in cities and towns throughout the state, each one boasting that it *sponsors* the best cookoff around.

 a.   is responsible for   b.   doesn't want   c.   refuses to have

3. The actual cooking for the competition is done in teams. The general requirement is that each group must cook *from scratch,* meaning no precooked or prepared ingredients.

   a. using foods prepared earlier

   b. outdoors

   c. starting from the beginning

4. Since the first cookoff, thousands have made the journey to Terlingua, some to compete and be judged, others just for the fun of watching the spectacle and eating their fill. In recent years, the enormous *turnout* has presented more than a few problems for the little ghost town.

   a. amount of food   b. number of people   c. city

5. Listed in this chapter are two recipes that you might *run across* in a Texas chili competition.

   a. find   b. visit   c. sell

III. Odd Man Out

Study the words in each group. Circle the word that is different.

Example: chef (waiter) cook   baker

In this case, *waiter* is the word that doesn't belong. A chef, a cook, and a baker all are involved in preparing the food, whereas a waiter serves it.

Example: beauty   contests   dancing   balloon rides (entertainment)

In this case, *beauty contests, dancing,* and *balloon rides* are all forms of *entertainment.*

1. spicy   sweet   salty   delicious

2. boast   realize   claim   announce

3. slice   cube   heat   chop

4. aficionado   fan   follower   winner

5. trophy   prize   medal   cash

6. contest   spectacle   championship   competition

7. peppers   garnish   celery   tomatoes

8. spices   garlic   cumin   oregano

IV. Word Forms

Put the correct form of the word in each blank. Check the verb forms for correct tense, number, and voice (active or passive), and check the nouns for number (singular or plural).

1. spice (n)   spicy (adj)
   a. I found the dish a little too _____.
   b. I couldn't find the _____ the recipe called for in the supermarket.

2. competition (n)   competitor (n)   compete (v)   competitive (adj)
   a. The two _____ in the original chili cookoff were H. Allen Smith and Daven Chasen.
   b. Athletes from all over the world come together to _____ in the Olympics.
   c. My little brother is extremely _____; if he doesn't get the highest grade in the class, he cries.
   d. Chili _____ are held in many states throughout the country.

3. spectacle (n)   spectator (n)   spectacular (adj)
   a. The circus performers dazzled the audience with their _____ feats.
   b. When the hometown team won, the _____ in the stadium cheered.
   c. The gathering of thousands of people from all over the world for the event was a _____ worth seeing.

4. consumer (n)   consumption (n)   consume (v)
   a. During the baseball game, the crowd _____ enormous amounts of hot dogs, popcorn, beer, and soda.
   b. There is a law requiring companies to provide _____ with a list of their products' ingredients.
   c. His doctor advised him to reduce his _____ of coffee and alcohol.

5. regulation (n)   regulate (v)
   a. A thermostat _____ the temperature of a room.
   b. There are _____ against swimming in that part of the lake.

6. subscription (n)   subscriber (n)   subscribe (v)

   a. Which magazines do you _____ to?

   b. I received a _____ to *Life* magazine for my birthday.

   c. The book club informed its _____ that it was going out of business.

7. alteration (n)   alter (v)

   a. His appearance _____ so much over the years that nobody at the re-union recognized him.

   b. We'll move into the apartment as soon as the _____ have been completed.

8. qualification (n)   qualify (v)   qualified (adj)

   a. They asked me what my _____ were for the job.

   b. I don't think he was _____ to teach that course; he didn't know enough about the subject matter.

   c. Her grades weren't high enough to _____ her for the scholarship.

V. Sentence Completion

Complete each sentence, using one of the words listed below.

      version   doses   sponsored   from scratch   gossip   staple   enhanced

1. It took her all day to prepare the meal because she cooked each dish _____ .

2. Nobody in the office trusted him because he was known as a _____ .

3. Rice is the _____ food in many countries in the world.

4. The additional spices _____ the flavor of the dish.

5. The church _____ a bake sale to raise money for their summer camp program.

6. Her doctor advised her not to take more than two _____ of the medicine a day.

7. I saw an earlier _____ of that movie many years ago.

COUNTERPARTS

1. Think of a festival or special event that you have attended. Record your ideas about the festival in the following chart:

Name of Festival: _____

Location (Where does it take place?)	
Purpose (What is this festival for?)	
Activities (What do people do?)	
Food (What do people eat?)	
Clothing (What do people wear?)	

Use your chart to tell a partner about the festival. Then write a descriptive paragraph about it to share with the rest of the class.

2. Chili is made with beef, one of the staples of the typical American diet. What are some of the staple foods in your native country? What are some commonly used spices? Describe some of the dishes made with these foods.

3. Have your own "food festival" by choosing one or more of the following activities.

   a. Bring in a dish that is native to your country.

   b. Write the recipe for your favorite dish and distribute it to the class.

   c. Try one of the recipes for chili suggested in the article.

Body Language Speaks Louder Than Words

1. How would you express the following ideas, using body language only? Compare ideas with your classmates.

- Be quiet.
- Come here.
- I'm listening to you.
- I agree with you.
- I don't understand.
- I don't know.

2. In the photograph above, one person is the employer (the boss) and one person is the employee. Based on their body language, can you tell which is which? How?

3. Think about the title of this chapter and look over the photographs in this chapter. Then tell what you think the article might be about.

I am a professional body watcher, and I love to turn others into body watchers, too. And that is precisely what I do in my university classes and in executive training seminars.

As a specialist in male-female communications, I propose that males and females in our culture speak different body languages. To illustrate this point I recruited Richard Friedman, Assistant to the President at the University of Cincinnati, to model with me for the accompanying photographs. The photos in which Friedman and I posed in our usual male and female roles, respectively, were easy. Then came the hard part, the part that proves my point. I posed us in postures° typical   body positions

Mills is famous for this pose, which she captions, "Could you say no to this woman?" In it she poses in a posture typical of the opposite sex.

of the opposite sex. The results in the photos illustrate the old maxim, "One picture is worth a thousand words."

The photos contain two basic sets of behavioral cues°— affiliative° cues and power cues. Male nonverbal behavior typically includes very few affiliative displays, such as smiles and head cants,° and many power cues, such as expanded limb positions and serious facial expressions. Female nonverbal behavior, however, is ordinarily just the opposite, containing many affiliative displays and few power cues. The overall impression males create is one of power, dominance,° high status, and activity, particularly in contrast to the overall impression females create, which is one of submission,° subordination, low status, and passivity.°

Sensitizing students and professional groups to these sex-role differences and the functions they serve in social and business contexts is my business. In my seminars, I illustrate how men spread out their upper and lower limbs, expanding to take up space; how men sit and stand in loose, relaxed postures; how they gesture widely, speak in loud, deep tones, and engage in either direct or detached eye-contact patterns. All these

signals
indicating a subordinate, or less
important position
head cants: tilted head positions

importance, authority

acceptance of someone else's power
inactivity

The author demonstrates another typical male pose. Women in business clothes appear shocking in this pose.

Friedman does not appear shocking in the same pose, since many business executives conduct business from a similar position.

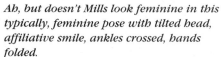

Ah, but doesn't Mills look feminine in this typically, feminine pose with tilted head, affiliative smile, ankles crossed, hands folded.

And doesn't Friedman look ridiculous in the same pose?

behaviors communicate power and high status, especially when men are communicating with subordinates. I also illustrate how women constrict° their arms and legs; sit in attentive, upright postures; gesture diminutively;° speak in soft, breathy voices; and lower their eyes frequently. These behaviors give away power and announce low status.

 In addition, I point out to audiences that women smile often, cant their heads, nod their heads, open their eyes in wide-eyed wonder, and posture themselves in positions of unstable balance. Men return smiles or not, at will,° engage in far less head canting and nodding, keep their eyes relaxed, and posture themselves in stable balance.

 Women in management are of particular concern to me. Managerial and professional women simultaneously play two roles, that of "woman" and that of "manager" (or professor, doctor, accountant, and so forth). And the role of woman and the role of manager or professional each has a different set of rules—contradictory° rules. From the depths of sex-role socialization comes the demand "be feminine," but from the context

make smaller or tighter with small movements

at will: as one wishes

opposing, conflicting

escape from a difficult situation

whole, undamaged

pronunciation

of the managerial work place comes the demand "be power-ful."

But there is a way for women to extricate° themselves and rise to the top of the corporate ladder with their femininity intact.° To succeed ultimately requires the simultaneous expression of both femininity and power. This involves a collapsing of the two inconsistent roles into a unified whole. The nonverbal behaviors of the women in this state include both messages of affiliation and power, delivered simultaneously. She smiles as she looks you straight in the eye. She spreads out her arms, cants her head, knits her brows in thought, and speaks with clear diction.°

And now a challenge: If you are a woman, assume the masculine poses pictured here; if you are a man, assume the female poses on these pages. By actually experiencing poses typical of those of the opposite sex, you may gain new insight into your own sex-role training—and learn to know a thing by its opposite.

Janet Lee Mills

EXERCISES

I.   Comprehension and Discussion Questions

General Ideas

1. What is the main idea of this article? What point does the writer try to prove?

2. According to the author of this article, how does the body language of females and males in the United States differ?

3. What does the author think a professional woman can do to appear both feminine and powerful?

Details

4. Scan the article to find answers to these questions:

    a. What is the author's profession?

    b. Who are the two people in the photographs?

    c. What are some examples of affiliative cues and power cues? List ideas from the reading in the chart on the next page.

Affiliative cues	Power cues
canting or tilting your head	*direct eye contact*

    d. What are the contradictory rules that professional women face?

Opinions
5. Look again at the photograph on page 112. Based on the information in the article, which person do you think is the boss? Why?

6. Based on her body language, what information is the woman in the photograph of page 113 communicating to you? Why?

7. Why do you think someone might attend one of the author's training seminars?

8. If you had a managerial position in the United States, would you change the way you use body language? If so, how?

II.   Between the Lines

Choose the answer that best completes each of the following statements based on the information in the article.

1.   In the United States, a woman using typical female body language is likely to appear

    a.   contradictory.   b.   passive.   c.   powerful.

2.   In American culture, lowering your eyes frequently and speaking in soft tones indicates that you are

    a.   listening carefully.   b.   subordinate.   c.   serious.

3.   When speaking with his employees, a male employer is likely to

    a.   speak loudly.   b.   tilt his head.   c.   look down.

4.   To succeed in business, this author thinks that a woman must

    a.   stop using affiliative cues.   b.   act like a man.   c.   use both affiliative and power cues.

5.   A woman can appear both feminine and powerful by

    a.   tilting her head and speaking softly.

    b.   using direct eye contact and maintaining a serious facial expression.

    c.   smiling and using direct eye contact.

III.   Vocabulary in Context

Find the italicized words below in the reading on pages 113–116. Use context to guess the meaning of each word. Then look up each word in a dictionary and choose the meaning that best fits the word in this context.

1.   Paragraph 1: *precisely*

    My guess: _____

    Dictionary definition: _____

2.   Paragraph 2: *respectively*

    My guess: _____

    Dictionary definition: _____

3.   Paragraph 3: *overall*

    My guess: _____

    Dictionary definition: _____

4. Paragraph 4: *limbs*

    My guess: _____

    Dictionary definition: _____

5. Paragraph 6: *simultaneously*

    My guess: _____

    Dictionary definition: _____

6. Paragraph 7: *inconsistent*

    My guess: _____

    Dictionary definition: _____

7. Paragraph 8: *assume*

    My guess: _____

    Dictionary definition: _____

IV. Word Forms

Put the correct form of the word in each blank. Check the verb forms for correct tense, number, and voice (active or passive), and check the nouns for number (singular or plural).

1. illustration (n)   illustrate (v)

    a. The author provided many examples to _____ her thesis that men and women use different body language.

    b. It will be easier for your audience to understand your ideas if you provide a few _____.

2. passivity (n)   passive (adj)   passively (adv)

    a. He's difficult to work with because he is so _____; it's hard to know what he is thinking or what he wants.

    b. Using only affiliative cues creates an impression of _____.

    c. He listened _____ to his employer's criticism, fearing that he would lose his job if he tried to defend himself.

3. dominance (n)   dominate (v)   dominant (adj)

    a. In a herd of horses, one horse will always establish _____ over the other horses.

    b. You can tell which horse in a herd is _____ by watching them eat. The _____ horse always gets to eat first.

    c. No one likes to spend time with her because she usually _____ the conversation.

4. impression (n)   impress (v)   impressive (adj)

    a. Although he is only fifteen years old, his knowledge of U.S. history is

        _____.

    b. If you want to make a good _____ at a job interview, you should dress
        appropriately.

    c. She worked long hours at her new job in an effort to _____ her boss.

5. relaxation (n)   relax (v)   relaxed (adj)

    a. Although he was nervous, he tried to sit in a _____ position.

    b. What do you do for _____ during the weekend?

    c. It's difficult to _____ when you are taking an important exam.

6. contradiction (n)   contradict (v)   contradictory (adj)

    a. No one believed his story because he gave _____ information.

    b. This morning she said that she was late for work because she was sick, but later she
        _____ herself by saying she had overslept.

    c. It's a _____ to say that you don't like sports but you like to play soccer.

V.   Sentence Completion

Complete each sentence, using one of the words listed below.

   contradicts   intact   dominate   passively   relax   impressed   behave   illustrate

1. The package arrived _____; nothing inside was broken.

2. She used photographs to _____ her ideas about body language.

3. One day he says that he wants a new job, but the next day he _____
    himself and says he wants to stay where he is.

4. My boss was so _____ with my work that I got a raise—and more work to
    do!

5. Sometimes it is hard to know how to _____ when you are living in a
    foreign culture.

6. The instructor won't allow one student to _____ the discussion because
    he wants everyone to have a chance to talk.

7. At the end of a hard day, she likes to _____ with a good book.

8. If you read an article without asking yourself questions, you are reading
    _____ rather than actively.

COUNTERPARTS

1. In your culture, do men and women use different body language? Give several examples to support your answer.

2. Try the challenge described in the last paragraph of the article. Then describe how you felt taking the pose of the opposite sex.

3. Choose several photographs of men and women from a magazine. See if their body language matches the typical male and female body language described in the article.

4. With a partner, role play a scene in which an employer and an employee interact at work. When you role play the scene for your classmates, use body language only. Ask your classmates to guess which person is the boss and tell why they think this.

Isamu Noguchi: Artist of Two Worlds

1. What outdoor sculptures are there in your area? Do you like them? Why or why not?

2. Read the title of this chapter. What do you think it means to be an "artist of two worlds"?

3. Read the first paragraph of the article and look at the pictures in this chapter. Then add your ideas to this chart.

What do you know about Noguchi?	What questions do you have about Noguchi?
He's an artist.	

ne of the ironies° of Isamu Noguchi's life was that in America he was considered a Japanese artist and in Japan he was regarded as American. In his autobiography,° he said of himself: "With my double nationality and my double upbringing,° where was my home? . . . Japan or America, either, both—or the world?" Although Noguchi never satisfactorily resolved this dilemma,° the Japanese-American sculptor had a long and successful career in both worlds. He integrated° the Eastern and Western aspects of his background and achieved international recognition as an artist.

conflicting things

one's life story
teaching of child

difficult problem

brought together, mixed

Noguchi was born in Los Angeles in 1904, the son of a Japanese poet, Yone Noguchi, and an American writer, Leoni Gilmour. He returned to live in Japan as a small child, but by then, his parents were separated and he saw little of his father. His mother, however, was a dominant° and affectionate influence in his early years; she was a woman of strong convictions and ideas, Noguchi wrote in his autobiography.

strong

When I was thirteen, my mother decided that I must go to America to continue my education. She had selected a school in Indiana that she had read about . . . . I am sure that she must have also been concerned about the unfortunate situation of children of mixed blood growing up in Japan of those days—half in and half out. She decided that I had better become completely American . . . . I was banished° as my mother decided.[1]

forced to leave

Noguchi finished high school in Indiana and was not reunited with his mother until she returned to the United States in 1923. It was with her encouragement that he enrolled° in art school in Greenwich Village to study sculpture. It was at this time that he took his father's last name of Noguchi; until

entered officially

then, he had been known as Isamu Gilmour. Noguchi quickly became involved in the active world of art of the 1920s in New York. In applying for a Guggenheim fellowship,° the young sculptor proposed that he study and travel for a period of three years, one in Paris and the other two in the Orient, explaining:

type of scholarship

> I have selected the Orient as the location for my produc-
> tive activities for the reason that I feel a great attachment for
> it, having spent half my life there. My father, Yone Noguchi,
> is Japanese and has long been known as an interpreter of the
> East to the West, through poetry. I wish to do the same
> with sculpture.[2]

Noguchi received the fellowship and left for France.

It was in Paris that he met and worked with one of the major influences in his life, the artist Constantin Brancusi. After his stay in France, Noguchi spent a portion of his time in Japan. There he had a strained° meeting with his father, who by this time had nine other children. When the artist finally returned to New York, he entered once again into the activities of the art world, exhibiting his work and pursuing a number of projects, including one for the building of a children's playground.

uncomfortable

Then, with the bombing of Pearl Harbor in 1941 Noguchi's life was dramatically altered. He said of the event, "Pearl Harbor was an unmitigated° shock, forcing into the background all artistic activities. With a flash I realized that I was no longer the sculptor alone, I was not just American but Nisei."° This new perception of his identity° led Noguchi to volunteer to enter one of the relocation camps in Arizona established for Japanese-Americans. One of his purposes in going there was to help design and develop recreational and park facilities for the camp. When he discovered that "the authorities wanted nothing permanent or pleasant," he attempted to leave. "But," he wrote, "it took me seven months to get out, and then only on a temporary basis." Of this experience, he later concluded, "The deep depression that comes with living under a cloud of suspicion, which we as Nisei experienced, lifted, and was followed by tranquility.° I was free finally of causes and disillusioned° . . . . I was resolved henceforth° to be an artist only."

absolute

second-generation Japanese-American
sense of self

calm/disappointed
from then on

Noguchi's long career as an artist was marked by a range and versatility that did not always bring him critical recognition. He did stage sets° and costumes for the dancer Martha

scenery

hanging lamps

a smooth, shiny stone/a dark, heavy metal

weathered the storm: lived through

Graham, designed playgrounds and gardens, created huge stone sculptures for the outdoors, and made delicate paper lanterns° and ceramics of simple beauty. He worked in almost every conceivable medium, including paper, marble,° bronze,° clay, wood, stainless steel, and, of course, stone, for which he is well known. This diversity was sometimes seen as a lack of seriousness or commitment to any one style. But Noguchi stated, early in his career, "I do not wish to belong to any one school. I am always learning, always discovering and changing. That I will not give up for the praise of some critic." Noguchi weathered the storm° of criticism; his many achievements are internationally admired. His designs of spaces can be seen across three continents: in America, Italy, France, Israel, and Tokyo. Of himself, Noguchi once said, "I am a very successful, unsuccessful sculptor."

One of the materials that Noguchi was always interested in working with is stone:"I love the use of stone because it is the most flexible° and meaning-impregnated° material. The whole world is made of stone .... It is as old as the hills." Noguchi's works in this element varied from the large, monolithic° pieces that graced his sculpture gardens and public places to the smaller pieces he did later in life. In 1982, he created a stone sculpture as part of a plaza he designed for the Japanese and American Center in Los Angeles. The sculpture is dedicated to the second-generation Japanese-Americans who, like Noguchi, faced the adversities° of being interned° during World War II.

After 1969, Noguchi divided his time between his house and studio on the Japanese island of Shikoku and his studio in Long Island City, New York. Many of his stone pieces were done in Japan, where he worked with local stonecutters. In New York, his studio served as a work place as well as a space to display outdoors some of his monumental sculptures. They weighed as much as three or four tons and were too heavy to be placed on any museum or gallery floor. Until his death in 1988, Noguchi continued to travel and work in both places. This dual aspect of his life and work was perhaps best summarized° by the art historian Sam Hunter in his book on Noguchi:

> The fact is that, while Noguchi did not feel entirely at home either in Japan or America, his artistic achievement shows him to be a citizen of the world, on a plane beyond nationality. He has turned the sense of nonbelonging, in fact, into a series of remarkably courageous . . . acts . . . and managed to combine in triumphant synthesis important features of both Eastern and Western traditions.[3]

*easily changed/**meaning-impregnated:** filled with meaning*

of one piece

difficulties/confined

explained in short form

---

[1]   From Isamu Noguchi, *A Sculptor's World* (New York: Harper & Row, 1968).

[2]   Ibid.

[3]   Sam Hunter, *Isamu Noguchi* (New York: Abbeville Press, 1978).

EXERCISES

I.   Finding the Facts: True or False?

Write *T* if the statement is true and *F* if it's false.

_____ 1.   Noguchi was born in Tokyo in 1904.

_____ 2.   The sculptor spent his childhood in Japan.

_____ 3.   He was the son of a Japanese father and an American mother.

_____ 4.   He came to live in the United States when he was in his early twenties.

_____ 5.   Noguchi voluntarily entered an internment camp for Japanese-Americans during World War II.

_____ 6.   While at the camp, he was able to design and develop recreational facilities.

_____ 7.   Noguchi enjoyed working in stone.

_____ 8.   During his adulthood, Noguchi rarely spent time in Japan.

II.   Between the Lines

Discuss the following questions.

1.   Reread the passage where Noguchi describes leaving Japan to come to the United States as a child. How do you think he felt at the time? Find the words or phrases that support your conclusion.

2.   Why did Noguchi choose the Orient as a place in which to work and study when he applied for a Guggenheim grant?

3.   How did Noguchi's experience in an internment camp during World War II affect his idea of himself as an artist?

4.   What do you think Noguchi meant when he described himself as a "very successful, unsuccessful artist?"

5.   At the end of the article, the writer of this article refers to the "dual aspect" of Noguchi's life and work. Explain this term.

III. Vocabulary in Context

Use context to choose the word or term that best fits the meaning of the italicized word in each sentence. Circle your answers.

1. "I am sure that she (my mother) must also have been concerned about the unfortunate situation of children of mixed blood growing up in Japan of those days—*half in and half out.*"

    a. unwanted   b. not fully accepted   c. uncomfortable

2. In applying for a Guggenheim fellowship, Isamu *proposed* that he study and travel for a period of three years, one in Paris and the other two in the Orient. Noguchi received the fellowship and left for France.

    a. presented his plan   b. refused the idea   c. accepted

3. Then, with the bombing of Pearl Harbor in 1941, Noguchi's life was dramatically *altered.* He said of the event, "Pearl Harbor was an unmitigated shock, forcing into the background all artistic activities. With a flash I realized that I was no longer the sculptor alone, I was not just American but Nisei."

    a. discovered   b. improved   c. changed

4. Noguchi's long career as an artist was marked by a range and *versatility* that did not always bring him critical recognition. He did stage sets and costumes, designed playgrounds and gardens, created huge stone sculptures, and made delicate paper lanterns.

    a. ability to do many things   b. repetition   c. wealth

5. Noguchi worked in almost every medium, including paper, marble, bronze, clay, wood, stainless steel, and, of course, stone. This *diversity* was sometimes seen as a lack of seriousness or commitment to any one style.

    a. commitment   b. variety   c. hard work

6. Noguchi's works in stone varied from the large, monolithic pieces that *graced* his sculpture gardens and public places to the smaller pieces he did late in life.

    a. decorated   b. enlarged   c. left

7. The fact is that, while Noguchi did not feel entirely at home either in Japan or America, his artistic achievement shows him to be a citizen of the world, on a *plane* beyond nationality.

    a. airplane   b. journey   c. level

IV.   Word Forms

Put the correct form of the word in each blank. Check the verb forms for correct tense, number, and voice (active or passive), and check the nouns for number (singular or plural).

1.   integration (n)   integrate (v)   integrated (adj)   integral (adj)

   a. Making errors is an _____ part of the learning process.

   b. She attended an _____ high school in the city.

   c. Community leaders demanded statewide _____ of the schools.

   d. Noguchi _____ both Eastern and Western traditions in his work.

2.   versatility (n)   versatile (adj)

   a. He's a _____ performer: he can sing, dance, and play several instruments.

   b. Noguchi's _____ caused some critics to believe that he was not a serious artist.

3.   banishment (n)   banish (v)

   a. The queen ordered the man to be _____ from the kingdom.

   b. News of his _____ outraged the townspeople.

4.   drama (n)   dramatic (adj)   dramatically (adv)

   a. Since the invention of the automobile, life has changed _____.

   b. The film was a _____ about a young couple whose child was dying of cancer.

   c. His entrance was very _____; he landed on the front lawn of the house in a helicopter.

5.   internment (n)   intern (v)

   a. The soldier _____ in a prisoner-of-war camp for two years during the war.

   b. Noguchi's _____ in a relocation camp for Japanese-American citizens lasted seven months.

6.   adversity (n)   adverse (adj)   adversely (adv)

   a. Despite the _____ conditions, the doctor decided to perform the operation.

   b. At first the patient reacted _____ to the doctor's advice, but later he decided that it was the best thing to do.

   c. She acted courageously in the face of _____.

7. product (n)   production (n)   produce (v)   productive (adj)

    a. When the company began advertising its _____ on television, sales went up.

    b. The company stopped _____ the drug when its harmful effects were discovered.

    c. The senator opposed an increase in the _____ of nuclear weapons.

    d. My weekend was very _____; I painted two rooms in my apartment and washed all the windows.

8. disillusionment (n)   disillusion (v)   disillusioned (adj)

    a. After a few years, he started to become _____ with his career.

    b. In her later writings, the author expressed her _____ with industrialized society.

    c. I don't want to _____ you, but I think you should be fully aware of the difficulties you will face.

V.   Sentence Completion

Complete each sentence, using one of the words listed below.

autobiography   indefinite   marble   sets   dilemma   infinite   monolithic   upbringing

1.   The top of the coffee table was made of _____.

2.   The actor's _____ included many amusing stories about famous Hollywood personalities.

3.   He can't resolve his _____ about which career to pursue.

4.   She designed the _____ for two award-winning plays.

5.   My grandmother is a person with _____ patience. Nothing seems to upset her.

6.   In reaction to his strict _____, he became rebellious as a teenager.

7.   Many people consider the _____ design of the building to be cold and impersonal.

8.   Because of the collapse of the bridge, train service has been discontinued for a(n) _____ period of time.

COUNTERPARTS

1. What is the attitude toward children of interracial marriages in your country? Are they generally accepted by society, or are they regarded, as Noguchi's mother thought he might be, as "half in and half out"?

2. Make a Venn Diagram comparing and contrasting Isamu Noguchi and Duane Hanson (or another artist). In the overlapping areas of the two circles, tell how the two artists are alike. In the outer areas of the circles, tell how they are different.

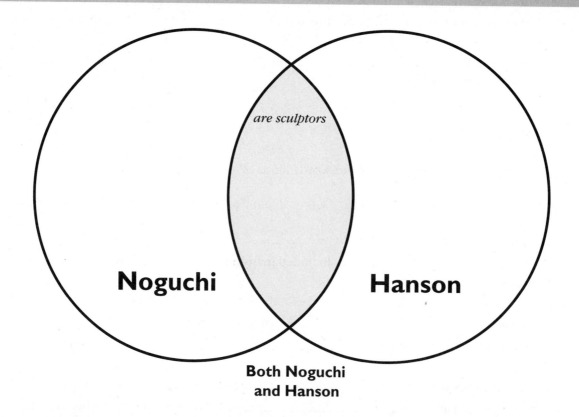

are sculptors

Noguchi   **Hanson**

**Both Noguchi
and Hanson**

Use your Venn Diagram to write about these two artists. In your writing, tell how they are alike and different.

3. When Noguchi was in his early twenties, he applied for a Guggenheim fellowship. In his application, he proposed to study and travel in France and Japan. An excerpt from his application appears on page 125. Imagine that you are applying for a grant to study and travel in another country. Write a brief proposal explaining where you would go and what you would study.

4. Explain how the events in Noguchi's life and the nature of his work contributed to the artist's conception of himself as a "man without a country."

The Story of the Shin's Family Store

© Harry Benson

1. Have you ever worked in a store? If so, what was your experience?

2. What do you think is involved in running a family store that sells fruit and vegetables? What everyday tasks does the family have to do?

3. Study the pictures in this chapter and read the first paragraph on page 135. Then list what you learned about Min Chul Shin.

A t 10 P.M., Min Chul Shin lowered the steel security gate over the front of the Fresh-N-Plus market, on Third Avenue near Seventy-eighth Street, and headed home with his wife. He ate some rice and took a shower. He put on a yellow knit shirt, blue jeans, and brown loafers and sat down in front of the television set to watch the news.

"I like to watch the news," Shin said.* "A lot of it I don't understand, but I like it. I also like *Star Wars* and science-fiction movies."

At midnight, just two hours after the end of the previous workday, Shin rose and grabbed° his blue nylon coat. He left his apartment and walked to his car. Sliding onto the front seat, he lit a cigarette. He put his foot on the accelerator° and headed for the New York City Terminal Market at Hunts Point. There, this twenty-seven-year-old Korean immigrant° would begin the ordeal° he undergoes° seven days a week.

"Everyday the same thing," Shin said. "It never change."

A few minutes later, Shin crossed the Willis Avenue Bridge. At the eastern fringe° of the South Bronx, Shin came to a chain-link fence.° He slowed, and the guard at the gate waved him into the 125-acre complex on the East River that handles more than half the fresh produce consumed° in this city. Oranges are trucked in from Florida. Artichokes arrive from California. Eggplants are shipped from Mexico. Strawberries are flown from New Zealand. The produce pours into the market from almost every state and from more than a dozen countries. And much of it is carried into the neighborhoods by Shin and his nine hundred or so fellow Korean retailers.° For just as the immigrant Greeks went into° coffee shops, the Pakistanis into newsstands, and the Israelis into taxicabs, the Koreans now dominate New York's retail produce business. Here, the only language is hard work, and this is a language in which Shin and his family are fluent.°

It was Shin's father who came to the United States first. He worked for two years until he had saved enough to send for his family. On February 28, 1974, Shin, his mother, his two sisters, and his two brothers boarded a plane for New York. The father

picked up

part of car that governs speed

foreigner who settles here
great difficulty/experiences

edge
chain-link fence: metal fence

eaten

store owners
went into: specialized in

very capable

*The quotations from Shin are in his own English.

was there at the airport with a friend who had a car. The friend drove the family around the edge of Manhattan.

"It was beautiful at night," Shin says. "The lights. In the day, not so beautiful. At night, beautiful." A month later, Shin landed° a $1.80-an-hour job at a printshop.° Most of the other men stopped work the minute the foreman° stepped out. Shin kept up a steady pace for twelve hours. He remembers, "No talking, only working. Maybe I born like that." The women in the office often made Shin do odd jobs.° "I'm very shy. I don't speak English."

The family settled in the Bronx, and Shin's brother David became the only Korean student at his junior high school. David recalls, "I didn't speak English, but I didn't feel any kind of shame, because I was younger. I usually make signs to make them understand." After school and on weekends, David worked at a fruit store in Queens. To make the trip, he had to ride the subway° for an hour and then hop a bus for thirty minutes. He says, "Nobody had any idea what a fruit store was. I come home and I say it was terrible hard work and I don't want to go back. They just smiled, laughed."

In mid-1974, an elderly Korean gentleman asked Shin's family to help him run a fruit stand in downtown Manhattan. Shin and his father worked in the back. David stood outside with a change counter and watched for thieves.° David says, "Then my family learn about the fruit business. Clean up, wash, cut it, wrap it, always work."

After a few months, the family began looking for a store of its own. To what they had made working for the elderly Korean gentleman, the father added what he had put away while working. Shin handed over° his savings from the printshop, and David contributed his wages from the fruit stand in Queens. The family picked up a lease° on a shop at West 147th Street and Broadway. On the first day, they sold one grapefruit.

"We know we have to do a lot of work," David says.

The family purchased a truck, and Shin paid fifty-four dollars for a four-hour driving course. He remembers, "I think the road test going to be easy. I take the test, and I fail." The second time he passed.

Early each morning, Shin and David climbed into the truck and drove to Hunts Point. Shin raced up and down the loading platforms. The four main warehouses° are broken down° into sixty-eight rooms leased by the city to the wholesalers.° The chambers swarmed° with men who carried in produce from

---

Margin glosses (left column):

got
place printing is done
person in charge of workers

odd jobs: chores

underground train

people who steal

handed over: gave

picked up a lease: rented

storage places/**broken down:** divided
those who sell to retailers
filled with great activity

the farms. In the midst of all this, Shin tried to find the best beans and the best cantaloupes and the best strawberries. He remembers, "I don't speak English. I only know 'How much?' and I count, 'One, two, three, four.'"

Some of the wholesalers grumbled° as Shin scrambled° over the mountains of produce, checking box after box for quality. Occasionally, a wholesaler slipped him a bad case. When there was a shortage, he often had to wait until the order of the other retailers had been filled. Shin says, "First time go to market, you could count with your fingers Korean people. They look down on Korean guy. Some items short, we don't get it. When it's left over, we get it."

complained/moved quickly

As Shin selected the produce, David loaded the truck. They usually left the market just after dawn. Shin dropped David off at Roosevelt High School and continued to the fruit store. When he stopped at a traffic light, he sometimes almost fell asleep. He remembers, "The eyes open, but the mind sleep." Then somebody would honk,° and Shin would snap back into the routine.° He would drive to West 147th Street, unload the truck, and begin another fifteen hours at the store.

press the car horn
usual way of doing things

© Harry Benson

"It never stop," Shin says. "No time to sleep. A lot of time I have no time to eat."

argument

In December 1976, the family learned that a feud° had broken out between two Korean brothers who owned a shop at West Eighty-fifth Street and Columbus Avenue. The younger brother was said to have left town, and the older brother was unable to run the business by himself. Shin's family sold its shop in Harlem and bought the business on the Upper West Side. Here people had more money. The family sold the produce at the 50 percent markup° standard in Korean fruit stores and learned that on a good day a shop could gross° $1,000 and net° about $200.

price increase
earn a total of
keep after expenses

One evening in 1977, Shin went to dinner at the home of another Korean fruit retailer. There he met a young woman named Sun. She had come from Seoul the year before, and she was working part time at a fruit store in Brooklyn. Shin encountered Sun again a few weeks later at the home of a friend. He ran into her a third time at a New Year's party. Sun remembers, "I see him at the party, and then, you know . . . . "

Grabbing moments between trips to the market and shifts at the store, Shin courted Sun. David remembers, "He have to be awake, because he try to get his wife." In February 1978, they were married. Now that Shin had a wife, his family gave him the money to start out on his own. David says, "The family work together first, and when it's time to get out, they help him to build up his family."

With five thousand dollars, Shin went in search of a good site for a fruit store. He walked up Third Avenue, and as he passed East Seventy-eighth Street he saw a closed store. He rang the bell of an upstairs apartment and learned that the space had been occupied by a hardware store that had gone out of business that same day. There was already a small fruit shop next door, but there seemed to be enough people strolling° along the avenue to support a second store.

walking slowly

In September, Shin and Sun opened the store. Shin took his brother's suggestion and called the store Fresh-N-Plus. There was some excitement when the first customer came in. The customer signed a dollar bill that Shin put on the wall as a good-luck charm.° Then Shin settled down to the same routine he had followed at the store on Columbus Avenue.

object believed to bring luck

"When you start, first couple months you feel dead," Sun says. "You feel numb° all the time."

unable to feel

The lucky dollar soon came down off the wall and went

toward buying produce. Most of the profits went back into the store, and as he expanded his inventory,° Shin was constantly picking up new ideas from other fruit-store owners. One owner discovered that green beans sold faster if he broke off the stem. Shin began breaking off the stem. Another owner started salvaging° the good sections of damaged melons and wrapping them in plastic. Shin began wrapping melons. He enclosed a plastic spoon.

list of things for sale

saving

"I learn every man have good idea," Shin says. "I pick them up and make them better."

Shin spent much of his time working in the back room. Sun served as the cashier° and salesperson. One customer brought her coffee in the morning. Another handed her a flower when she looked depressed. Other customers were not so pleasant. One day, a man bought a *TV Guide* and came back a few minutes later, complaining that the pages were loose. He threw the magazine in Sun's face. Sun remembers, "He said, 'Go back to your country.' I said, 'You should go back to your country, too.'"

person who takes payments

There were also more than a few shoplifters.° One day, Sun was forced to confront a man in a business suit who had slipped a tomato in his pocket. Sun says, "Even ladies steal."

people who steal from stores

By this time, the father was growing older, and David began running the store on Columbus Avenue. He and Shin agreed to share a truck and hire an American driver. A cousin named Choi arrived from Korea, and Shin put him to work in the store. With this added help, Shin could sometimes take a few minutes off for a cup of coffee. "Now it is easy," Shin says.

But even after several years, Shin's routine is much the same as it was the first day he went to work in the market. The Monday of Thanksgiving week was a typical day. Shin arrived at Hunts Point at 12:35 A.M. and parked his station wagon.° He went up some steps and walked onto the loading platform. Soon Shin met up with David. They exchanged nods and went over to the clerk. Shin bought fourteen boxes of strawberries at $2.75 a pint. He asked the price of broccoli, and the clerk said the truck had not arrived from Florida. Shin asked, "What time come?" The clerk answered, "When it comes." David inquired about artichokes. There had been too much rain in California, and the price had jumped from the usual $8 a box to $25 a box.

station wagon: type of large car

"Everything high," David said. "Bad weather in California or Florida, price here go up right away."

As he was leaving, he stopped to ask about bunches of carrots. Shin said, "Talk to me." The clerk said, "How can I? I don't speak Korean."

a Chinese food

proof of payment

"Hey, Egg Roll,° you all look alike, you know that?" a porter shouted at Shin. The cashier handed him a receipt° made out to "Egg Roll."

substitute name (usually friendly)

"Just a nickname,"° Shin said.

Shin and David continued along the platform. Asparagus was going for $45 a box, twice the usual price. David said, "Sometime you don't make any profit on an item, but you still have to have it or lose customers." Shin said, "Customer fill two basket, don't see one item need, leave. Most important thing to have good items. That is how keep customers."

running

After five hours of scurrying° from storeroom to storeroom, Shin was done. He walked into the nearby coffee shop and said, "Breakfast," to the cook. A minute later, the cook handed him a paper plate containing two fried eggs and French fries.

Dawn found Shin crossing the Third Avenue bridge into Manhattan.

At 6:50 A.M. he parked his station wagon in front of the Fresh-N-Plus market. He pulled his jacket over his shoulders and smoked a cigarette.

carrying

A few minutes later, his cousin Choi arrived from the Bronx. With him was a young man named Pak, who had been in New York just six months. Shin, Choi, and Pak began lugging° produce out of the cooler at the back of the store. Shin sat down on a plastic five-gallon can. He spilled some green beans on the table and began sorting. He threw the spotted beans on the floor, and he ripped the stems off the good beans. He has learned he can get a few pennies more for the smaller beans, and he put these to the side. In forty minutes he cleaned twenty-five pounds.

"I don't eat beans," Shin said.

sat on her heels/box

At 11 A.M., Sun appeared. The truck arrived from the market, and it took two hours to unload and store the produce. Deciding to take a nap, Shin lay down in the back room. Sun squatted° by the sink with a crate° of parsley. As she separated the green ones from those that were dry, Sun spoke of her high-school days in Korea.

"That's the time in life," Sun said. "You don't worry making living. You think everything is for yourself and you could do everything you want. But that's not true."

in-house phone system

Over the intercom,° the cashier reported that the line of

© Harry Benson

customers was getting long. Sun ran out and worked the second register for a few minutes. A man in a gray suit came up and asked, "Are these your best grapefruit?" Sun said they were, and she returned to the parsley. She hunched° her shoulders and said that her back hurt.

bent

"I must be getting old," Sun said. "We want to get out of this as soon as possible, but what can you do? If you want to live in New York, sometimes you have to be tough."

The intercom summoned Shin to shoo° away a man who looked like a shoplifter. As Shin headed back, a woman asked him if he carried 60-watt light bulbs. Shin climbed up to an upper shelf and grabbed a box of two.

send, scare

"Can I buy only one?" the woman asked.

"Okay," Shin said.

Then Shin returned to the back room and cleaned a crate of leaf lettuce, slipping each head into a plastic bag. "Very tender," Shin said. This done, he lugged a box of iceberg lettuce out of the cooler. The telephone rang, and Shin stopped to talk to his brother.

"He want to know what time to go to market," Shin said. "I say same as today."

Shin continued without pause until 9:30 P.M. He then rolled the racks of fruits and vegetables off the sidewalk and carried the produce back into the freezer. After he locked the security gate, he checked his watch and saw that it was 10:04 P.M. In one hour and fifty-six minutes it would be time to leave for the market.

EXERCISES

I.   Comprehension and Discussion Questions

General Ideas
1.   How did Shin and his family learn the produce business?

2.   What are some of the problems Shin encounters running his business, both at the produce warehouse and in his store?

3.   What are some of the things that Shin and his wife have to do every day as owners of a small grocery store?

4.   How has Shin's life changed in the years he has been in the United States?

Details
5.   Scan the reading to find answers to these questions:

   a. When did Shin come to the United States?

   b. What was Shin's first job in the United States?

   c. Who is David?

   d. Where is Shin's store?

   e. On a typical workday, when does Shin usually get up?

Opinions
6.   What do you think is the purpose of this article?

7.   Do you think Shin enjoys his work? Give examples from the reading to support your opinion.

8.   What do you think is the most difficult thing about running the Fresh-N-Plus market?

9.   Shin said that the wholesalers looked down on him. What examples does he give to support this idea? Why do you think the wholesalers acted in this way?

II.   Sequencing Exercise

Number the events of the story in the order in which they occurred.

_____   a.   Shin and his family worked for an elderly owner of a fruit stand in downtown Manhattan.

_____   b.   Shin met Sun at the home of a friend, and a year later they were married.

_____   c.   Shin's father came to the United States and worked for two years before sending for his family.

_____   d.   The Shin family opened their own fruit store in Harlem.

_____   e.   Shin, his brother David, another brother, his two sisters, and his mother arrived in the United States and settled in the Bronx.

_____   f.   While his brother David worked weekends in a fruit store in Queens, Shin had a low-paying job in a printshop.

_____   g.   A second fruit store was purchased by the Shin family in a prosperous neighborhood.

_____   h.   With money given to him by his family, Shin opened his own fruit store on Manhattan's Upper East Side.

III.   Between the Lines

Choose the answer that best completes each of the following sentences.

1.   Shin begins his workday
     a. in the evening.   b. in the morning.   c. in the middle of the night.

2.   According to the article Shin averages about _____ hours of sleep a night.
     a. eight   b. five   c. two

3.   When Shin is at the produce market, he examines the produce in each crate carefully because
     a. sometimes the crates are empty.
     b. he wants to count the produce in each crate.
     c. he has been sold poor-quality produce in the past.

4.   Shin's family bought their second produce store on the West Side because
     a. they could make more money there.
     b. they wanted to help out the owner.
     c. Shin's father and brother were having a feud.

5. Shin took his "lucky dollar" off the wall because

    a. a customer asked for it.

    b. he needed it to expand his inventory.

    c. he was afraid someone would steal it.

6. Shin's work is a little easier now because

    a. he can take coffee breaks.

    b. he has more people to help him.

    c. there is less shoplifting.

7. When the clerk at the wholesale warehouse calls Shin "Egg Roll," his attitude is

    a. sympathetic.   b. complimentary.   c. insulting.

8. Shin's wife, Sun, feels that she and her husband

    a. should work harder.

    b. are very satisfied with their life.

    c. have a difficult life.

IV. Vocabulary in Context

Use context to choose the word or term that best fits the meaning of the italicized words in each sentence. Circle your answers.

1. A month later, Shin landed a $1.80-an-hour job at a printshop. Most of the other men stopped work the minute the foreman *stepped out.* Shin kept up a steady pace for twelve hours.

    a. entered   b. left the room   c. walked faster

2. After school and on weekends, David worked at a fruit store in Queens. To make the trip, he had to ride the subway for an hour and then *hop* a bus for thirty minutes.

    a. jump over   b. stop   c. get on

3. After a few months, the family began looking for a store of its own. To what they had made working for the elderly Korean gentleman, the father added what he had *put away* while working.

    a. spent   b. saved   c. lost

4. One evening in 1977, Shin went to dinner at the home of another Korean fruit retailer. There he met a young woman named Sun. Shin *encountered* Sun again a few weeks later at the home of a friend.

    a. met   b. named   c. married

5. With five thousand dollars, Shin went in search of a good *site* for a fruit store. He walked up Third Avenue, and as he passed East Seventy-eighth Street he saw a closed store.

    a. amount of money   b. noise   c. place

6. Shin was constantly picking up new ideas from other fruit-store owners. One owner discovered that green beans sold faster if he *broke off* the stem. Shin began breaking off the stem.

    a. damaged   b. removed   c. sold

7. Shin sat down on a plastic five-gallon can. He spilled some green beans on the table and began *sorting*. He threw the spotted beans on the floor, and he ripped the stems off the good beans.

    a. separating things   b. eating   c. walking around

V.   Word Forms

Put the correct form of the word in each blank. Check the verb forms for correct tense, number, and voice (active or passive), and check the nouns for number (singular or plural).

1. accelerator (n)   acceleration (n)   accelerate (v)

    a. The _____ in my car needs adjustment.

    b. The cyclist _____ as he neared the finish line.

    c. The pilot increased _____ as she took off.

2. fluency (n)   fluent (adj)   fluently (adv)

    a. A month in Brazil really improved my _____ in Portuguese.

    b. She is _____ in three languages.

    c. I used to speak Russian _____, but now I can hardly form a sentence.

3. stroller (n)   stroll (v)

    a. The young couple _____ down the street arm in arm.

    b. The two _____ stopped to watch the children playing in the park.

4. expansion (n)   expand (v)   expansive (adj)

    a. The _____ of the store was necessary but expensive.

    b. After a few years, they _____ the house by adding two rooms.

    c. Because of his _____ personality, he is a lot of fun to be with.

5. contribution (n)   contributor (n)   contribute (v)

    a. Your _____ to the project was greatly appreciated.

    b. The nonprofit organization sent letters to all of its _____.

    c. The senator thanked everyone who _____ to the success of her campaign.

VI. Synonyms

From the list below, choose synonyms for the italicized words and phrases.

make it   ordeal   go into   site   landed a job (with)   lug   grabbed   grumbled

1. We couldn't find a taxi in the pouring rain, so we had to *drag* our suitcases to the bus station ourselves.

2. After the plane crash, the sole survivor had been stuck on a mountaintop for days. The reporters were eager to ask him questions about his *difficult experience.*

3. The owner of the shop *complained under his breath* whenever one of his employees took a long lunch hour.

4. The thief suddenly *seized* the woman's pocketbook and fled.

5. The company spent several weeks looking for a good *location* for their new factory.

6. It is difficult to *become successful* in New York because the competition is fierce.

7. After eight frustrating months of looking for work, Sam *was hired by* an ad agency.

8. After majoring in math in college, Alice decided *to enter the field of* computers.

COUNTERPARTS

1. Do you know anyone who runs a small business? If so, what kind of business is it? What is their everyday schedule like? What kinds of problems do they face? In writing, describe this small business.

2. In small groups, list the advantages and disadvantages of running a family business. Write your group's ideas in the chart on the next page.

Running a family business

Advantages	Disadvantages
you make the decisions	*long hours*

Would you like to run a family business? Explain your answer in writing. Use the chart above for ideas.

3. When Shin first arrived in the United States, he worked in an office for very low wages. Because he didn't speak English, he was sometimes taken advantage of by some of his co-workers. Have you ever had an experience where you were taken advantage of because you did not know English? Describe the experience.

4. Imagine that you own a fruit and vegetable store. In a small group, list the ten most important things that you would do to be successful. Then compare lists with another group.

Protecting the Environment

1. In your opinion, what are the most serious environmental problems in the world today? What are the causes of these problems? List your ideas in a chart.

Environmental problems	Causes
air pollution	*too many cars, pollution from factories*

2. The pictures in this chapter show the actions some people are taking to protect the environment. Study the pictures and tell what you think these people are doing.

3. Read the first sentence in each paragraph on page 149. What do you think this article is about? What questions do you have about the topic? Share ideas with your classmates.

reenpeace is the world's largest environmental group. Between 1980 and 1990, membership in this organization increased from 240,000 to 1.6 million in the United States. Worldwide the group has 2.5 million members.

Greenpeace members have risked their lives by placing themselves in small boats between whales and the harpoon guns of whaling ships. Its members have dangled° from a New York bridge to protest a barge carrying garbage out to sea, skydived from the smokestacks of coal-burning power plants to protest acid rain,° sneaked into plants to document illegal pollution, and led countless demonstrations.°

hung

acid rain: rainwater that is made more acidic by factory smoke

public expressions of an opinion

taking an active role; aggressive

threatening

within the system: by changing the laws

destroying

civil disobedience: refusing to obey laws thought to be wrong or unfair

using a substance to change the color of

put your life on the line: risk your life

Two environmental groups that are even more activist° than Greenpeace are Earth First! and the Sea Shepherd Conservation Society. These two organizations use aggressive° tactics because their members believe that the earth can't wait for the beneficial, but much too slow, pace of change accomplished by working only within the system.° Their goals are to prevent environmental destruction, increase citizen awareness, and raise the costs of business for loggers, whalers, and others practicing planet wrecking.°

These two environmental groups practice civil disobedience° and aggressive nonviolence. This means *absolute nonviolence* against humans and other living things and *strategic violence* against inanimate objects such as bulldozers, power lines, and whaling ships. Tactics include chaining themselves to the tops of trees to keep loggers from cutting them down; driving spikes into trees and labeling these trees (the spikes don't hurt the trees, but they break sawblades, which could hurt loggers or millworkers, so the trees are labeled to keep them from being cut down); blocking bulldozers with their bodies; blocking or sinking illegal whaling ships; felling high-voltage towers; and dyeing° the fur of harp seals to prevent them from being killed for their furs.

Members of activist environmental groups point to the long history of civil disobedience against laws believed to be unjust—the American Revolution, the fight to allow women to vote, the civil rights movement, the antiwar movement, and now the environmental movement. Benjamin White, Jr., Atlantic Director of the Sea Shepherd Conservation Society, summarizes why we must all become environmental activists:

> *We must begin by declaring a state of planetary emergency . . . . We must stop compromising our basic right to clean air, water, soil, and bloodstreams, and a future with wild animals and wilderness . . . . We must also be willing to take risks. If your family were threatened, would you put your life on the line?° Would you go to jail if necessary? Your family is threatened. It's time to take direct action.*

An increasing number of ordinary citizens are directly or indirectly supporting activist environmental groups because they fear for their children's environmental future. They are fed up

with presidents and other politicians who make nice speeches about protecting the environment and behind the scenes allow the continuing rape° of the earth in the name of short-term economic growth.

destruction

In 1988, a Kansas woman who lived near Wichita's Vulcan Chemical plant and whose family had been beset with health problems handcuffed herself to a chair outside the governor's office until he saw her. In 1989, protesters of Conoco, Inc., a refinery° in Ponca City, Oklahoma, set up a tent city on the grounds of the state capitol in 1989. In 1990, Conoco offered the families who lived near the refinery up to $27 million to relocate.

a factory that refines or purifies oil

In 1989, a social studies class at a New Jersey high school persuaded the school board to switch from Styrofoam lunch trays to old-fashioned washable dishes. Since then, these students have protested McDonald's recycling practices and are raising money to buy and protect 121 hectares (300 acres) of rain forest in Belize.

nipping at their heels: pushing or forcing them

Environmentalists disagree over the tactics used by activist groups. Some applaud and join or financially support these activist groups. Some point out that leaders of mainstream environmental groups need to have activist groups nipping at their heels° to make them take stronger positions.

negative reaction

seek to influence lawmakers to pass certain laws

Other environmentalists fear that activist groups, especially if they begin using illegal or violent actions, could cause a public backlash° against other environmental efforts and groups. Some worry that if activists alienate the public and Congress, industry will be able to successfully lobby° Congress to rewrite and weaken environmental laws. What do you think?

EXERCISES

I.   Comprehension and Discussion Questions

General Ideas

1.   What is the purpose of Greenpeace, Earth First!, and the Sea Shepherd Conservation Society?

2.   Why do some environmental groups practice strategic violence against nonliving things? What are some of the tactics they use?

3.   Some people think the tactics of the more activist environmental groups might hurt the environmental movement. How?

Details

4.   Scan the reading to find answers to the questions below.

   a.   Who is Benjamin White, Jr.? Why is he quoted in this article?

   b.   How did Conoco, Inc. respond to protesters who set up a tent city at the Oklahoma state capitol?

   c.   What are students at a New Jersey high school raising money for?

Opinions

5.   Why do you think that members of Greenpeace engage in dangerous activities such as skydiving and dangling from a bridge?

6.   Do you agree with Benjamin White's ideas quoted in the reading? Why or why not?

7.   Do you think that activist groups such as Earth First! and the Sea Shepherd Conservation Society serve a useful role? Why or why not?

8.   What is your response to the question at the end of the reading?

II.   **Vocabulary in Context**

Use context to choose the word or term that best fits the meaning of the italicized word in each sentence. Circle your choice.

1.   Members of Greenpeace have dangled from a New York bridge to protest a *barge* carrying garbage out to sea.

    a. large boat   b. large car   c. demonstration

2.   Some environmental groups practice strategic nonviolence against *inanimate* objects such as bulldozers, power lines, and whaling ships.

    a. living   b. nonliving   c. useless

3.   In 1989, a social studies class at a New Jersey high school persuaded the school board to *switch* from Styrofoam lunch trays to old-fashioned washable dishes.

    a. eat   b. change   c. take

4.   Since then, these students have protested McDonald's recycling practices and are *raising* money to buy and protect 121 hectares of rain forest in Belize.

    a. collecting   b. selling   c. losing

5.   An increasing number of citizens are *fed up with* presidents and other politicians who make nice speeches about protecting the environment and behind the scenes allow the continuing rape of the earth in the name of short-term economic growth.

    a. encouraged by   b. happy with   c. tired of

III.   **Checking the Facts: True or False?**

Write *T* if the sentence is true and *F* if the sentence is false.

_____ 1.   All environmental groups practice civil disobedience.

_____ 2.   Members of the environmental organization Earth First! practice strategic violence against people and things.

_____ 3.   Greenpeace members use more aggressive tactics than members of the Sea Shepherd Conservation Society.

_____ 4.   Civil disobedience is a new strategy for protesting unfair laws.

_____ 5.   Some environmentalists think that aggressive tactics will have a negative effect on the environmental movement.

_____ 6.   Demonstrating against acid rain is an example of strategic violence against inanimate objects.

Rewrite the false statements to make them true.

IV.   Word Forms

Put the correct form of the word in each blank. Check the verb forms for correct tense, number, and voice (active or passive), and check the nouns for number (singular or plural).

1.   demonstration (n)   demonstrate (v)
    a. Many people carried signs when they _____ against the war.
    b. During the _____ against the war, hundreds of people marched through the center of town.

2.   environment (n)   environmental (adj)
    a. Some people feel that we are not doing enough to protect the _____.
    b. Some _____ groups use aggressive tactics in hopes of increasing citizen awareness.

3.   success (n)   succeed (v)   successful (adj)
    a. If you want to be _____ in your job, you should keep up with new developments in the field.
    b. By lying down on the road, the protesters _____ in stopping the bulldozers.
    c. The tent city demonstration was a _____; after two years, the company agreed to pay families to relocate.

4.   risk (n, v)   risky (adj)
    a. If you want to be successful in business, you must be willing to take
        _____.
    b. He _____ his life when he ran into the burning building to save the child.
    c. It is _____ to invest in a new business. You could lose all your money.

5.   destruction (n)   destroy (v)   destructive (adj)
    a. Benjamin White, Jr. believes that everyone should work to prevent the _____ of the Earth.
    b. Acid rain is very _____; it can kill trees, plants, and animals.
    c. _____ the rain forests will have a negative effect on the earth's atmosphere.

6. protection (n)   protect (v)   protective (adj)

   a. In some jobs, workers must wear _____ clothing such as hard hats and face masks.

   b. You should wear a seat belt when you are in a car. It's for your own

       _____.

   c. In the past twenty years, a number of laws have been passed to _____ the environment.

V.   Sentence Completion

Complete each sentence using one of the words listed below.

    dyed   illegal   relocated   risky   sneaked   unjust   wrecked

1. During the night, several people _____ into the factory to copy important documents. No one saw them enter or leave the factory.

2. He _____ his gray hair black so that he would look younger.

3. She refused to obey the law because she felt it was _____.

4. It's very _____ to skydive from the smokestack of a coal-burning factory.

5. She _____ her car in the accident but no one got hurt.

6. In the United States, it is _____, or against the law, for people under the age of 21 to buy alcohol.

7. He couldn't find a job in Miami, so he _____ to New York.

COUNTERPARTS

1. Interview several people outside of class. Find out what they consider to be the most serious environmental problems in the world today. Together with your classmates, graph the results of your interviews.

2. Find out about an environmental issue of importance today. Look up the word *environment* in a library's copy of the *Reader's Guide to Periodical Literature.* Choose an article that interests you, read it, and tell the class what you learned.

3. Choose an environmental problem of interest to you. Design a series of signs that people could carry in a demonstration to bring attention to this problem.

4.   Demonstrations are a nonviolent way to express your opposition to something. Have you ever seen or participated in a demonstration? What was your experience? Do you think demonstrations are an effective way to express opinions? Why or why not?

Vietnam Veterans Memorial: The Debate

1. Describe a war memorial that you have seen. How is it similar to or different from the war memorial above.

2. The pictures on pages 158 and 163 show the Vietnam Veterans Memorial in Washington D.C. Based on the pictures, how would you describe this memorial? Share ideas with your classmates.

3. Look over pages 159–166. How is this reading organized? How is it different from the other readings in this book?

CHAPTER 15

*On November 16, 1982, one hundred thousand people gath-
ered in Washington, D.C., to dedicate° a memorial to Americans who died in Vietnam. The funds to put up the monument had been raised by veterans of the war. The design was
selected from entries° in a national competition, which had
been judged by a committee of experts in the fields of art and
architecture. The winning entry—a slab° of black granite°
inscribed with the names of those who had died in Vietnam—
immediately stirred up controversy.° Some attacked the
modern architectural style as inappropriate;° others found it
a particularly fitting choice for a memorial. The arguments
were heated, reviving emotions over a conflict that had
divided the nation. The following excerpts reflect a range of
reactions, both pro and con. They were written by newspaper
and magazine reporters, architects, and authors; the final one
is by a man who is a veteran of Vietnam.*

offically open

works submitted

large, flat piece/a type of
hard rock

difference of opinion
not proper

From *New Republic*

ow do you have a memorial for this sort of thing? Seven
million dollars were raised for it and the winning design was that of Maya Yang Lin, a young Yale architecture student. The contestants were instructed only that their
entries should display the names of the fallen "without political or military content." I think it is one of the most impressive
memorials I ever saw . . . .

It is an outdoor affair. As you approach the monument,
you come up a walk bent to make a long V, each side of which
is 250 feet long. The meadow° is on one side, and the polished
granite slabs are on the other. The slabs have names on them;
they are sunk into a gentle hill. It is the names that do it. They
are not listed by rank or alphabet, but in the order of their
deaths. These were eager young men fighting in the jungles°
of Vietnam. Sometimes they thought they knew what they
were doing; often they were confused. Now the names are
there—Leland G. Deeds, Imlay S. Swiddeson, Richard M. Seng—

field

thick forests

but take your eye off them, and you can't find the place again. It's just names, people, you and me and our sons. There are no inscriptions° to tell you what to think; there are no heroic utterances.° It is stark.° Each name is a special boy who never came home. It is all left to the observer. The dark, shining slabs of granite are as hard and polished as a mirror, and you can see your image reflected over the names as you lean forward. My eyes moistened. In the crowd, we looked at each other, deeply moved.

written indications
statements/severe

From Tom Wolf in *The Washington Post*

shocked/very angry

Veterans . . . were dumbfounded° and then outraged.° Far from "honoring" and "recognizing" those who served in Vietnam, the Lin design simply buried the idea of Vietnam, put them in a pit, below ground, in funereal° black, as part of something too horrible and shameful to be mentioned by name or even associated with the American flag.

deathlike

The Lin design ruled out any flag; and nowhere on the memorial was any reference to be made to the war in Vietnam. Visitors were to walk down into the pit and come upon a black wall bearing the names of fifty-seven thousand dead men (and a few women)—with no explanations as to how, much less why, such a dreadful sacrifice took place . . . .

The veterans could have gotten any kind of sculpture they wanted—since they paid for the memorial with money they raised by themselves—had they not come up with the bright° idea of turning the choice over to a jury of art experts.

clever

Most veterans who wanted a Vietnam war memorial entertained no hopes of refighting that battle. But they did want to remove the stigma° from men who, as they saw it, had served their country—honorably. They kept talking about a memorial "to honor and recognize those who served in Vietnam"; and, indeed, that phrase was written into the congressional order authorizing the veterans to erect the memorial on a choice stretch of Capitol-Hill park land between the Lincoln Memorial and the Washington Monument.

bad reputation

Most of them, if the truth be known, had only a passing interest in "remembering the dead." They wanted to remove the big accusing index finger° from those who had returned from Vietnam and were living in its shadow.

index finger: *finger next to thumb*

They had in mind a statue, like the Iwo Jima Memorial of the Second World War or the Grand Army Plaza memorial of the Civil War.

From *Vogue*

It seems to me that Maya Lin's monument has been assaulted° largely because it is out of character. Most people can scarcely imagine a monument without statues; to build one outside this convention° seems a provocation. Many Vietnam veterans were surely especially sensitive to the fact that the memorial is an exception. They wanted it built precisely to establish a connection with veterans from other wars. But beyond the simple fact of commemoration,° there is also the undeniable fact that it is not the kind of war memorial that is a memorial to war—no charging GIs with bayonets° . . . .

The final reason that had Maya Lin's (male) critics in such a dither° was undoubtedly that the source of this modernism was not simply a student, not simply an Oriental, but worst of all, a woman. That a woman—the ultimate outsider—should have won the commission was the final affront,° absolute confirmation that the war was to be remembered differently, a monument emasculated.° How could a woman, from her perspective° outside of (male) history, be expected to place the Vietnam war within the stream of that history.

Perhaps it was Maya Lin's "otherness" that enabled her to create such a moving work. Perhaps only an outsider could have designed an environment which is so successful in answering the need for recognition by a group of people—the Vietnam vets—who are plagued by a sense of "otherness" forced on them by a country that has spent ten years pretending not to see them. Women have been invisible a lot longer than that. Maya Lin has been able to make a memorial that doesn't insult the memory of the war by compromising the fact of its difference. She knows that honest memories are the strongest. For that reason, the Vietnam memorial is likely to retain its power over the emotions long after private memories of the war have faded.

attacked

traditional way of doing things

honoring a memory

guns with knives attached

state of excitement

insult

made less powerful
way of seeing something

From *Art News*

The designer—who was too young to be involved in the politics of the Vietnam era—said, "It's a memorial to other human beings; to the people who served, to those who died and to those who lost people." She cites° as primary models European memorials constructed after the First World War, especially one in France, where the experience of walking into or through the memorial provides the stimulus° for reflection.

gives an example

inspiration

From *The National Review*

Experienced directly, however, rather than in theory, the memorial possesses considerable power and even eloquence.° Much of this comes from its high-gloss° surface, on which both the Lincoln Memorial and the Washington Monument reflect—suggesting, if you wish, some of the ideals for which the men fought and died, and also joining their monument to American history itself. The spectator,° moreover, sees his own reflection superimposed° on the carved names, symbolically uniting him to them. Miss Lin has not only a sense of design, but a sense of design-it-its site, and she has created something unusual and beautiful.

ability to persuade
shiny

observer
placed over

From *The New York Times*

Each day more than ten thousand people, coming at all hours of day and night, walk past the glossy black marble wall on which are carved the names of 57,939 Americans who died in Vietnam. In the number of visitors it attracts, according to the National Park Service, the war monument is second only to the Lincoln Memorial, a nearby symbol of another war that divided the country.

But in one sense, the Vietnam Memorial, in the earth, is like no other in the nation's capital. Even the children, who can be seen playing around other Washington landmarks, fall quiet as they approach the V-shaped wall that bears the grief of mothers, fathers, widows, children, comrades, and friends.

And, as they have done from the first day, many of the visitors indulge in° the simplest human memorial, touching the cold, stony texture° of the engraved° names of the dead. For

indulge in: allow themselves
how a surface feels/cut into

them, it is not enough just to read the names. They must touch them, even at night, when they show up by flashlight° and in the flickering° glow of matches struck in the dark.

handheld electric light
unsteady

There is something new these days. Some visitors place a piece of paper over a name and rub a pencil over it. Then they take the rubbing back home to some next of kin° who has not yet made the journey to Washington.

next of kin: family member

These scenes are particularly distressing for the Park Service volunteers who are stationed at the memorial to assist visitors in finding names.

One of them, Elaine Shriber, on the job only a few weeks, said every day was like the first. "Some don't want any help in finding the name," she said, "so I always step back and let them be. They want to be alone." Referring to Vietnam veterans who come looking for the names of comrades, Mrs. Shriber said, "The buddies are the ones that stand out. They stare at the names the longest, rubbing the letters with their fingers and trying not to cry, but nearly always breaking down."°

breaking down: losing control

Gertrude Gerber, who has been working as a volunteer since she retired from her job at the Department of Commerce, said, "A lot of the people I help are here to take pictures of the

names or to do rubbings that they can take back home to somebody who lost a son or brother in Vietnam. They cry and we cry with them. I go home at times and tell my husband about it and start crying again" . . .

The impact of the wall is felt even by those who never served in Vietnam or lost a family member there. John Armstrong, fifteen years old, a blond-haired boy in a red T-shirt and blue jeans, was looking for the name of a friend's brother. The youth, who is from Oakville, Missouri, was seven years old

In 1984, a statue of three soldiers was placed 100 yards away from the Vietnam Veterans Memorial. It was hoped that this more traditional statue would help to end the debate over the memorial.

impressive

when the war ended. He said, "I just want to go home and tell him that I found his brother's name. It's really awesome.° I had seen the wall on television, but it's different when you walk up to those names."

From *Newsweek*

Those who think the war was folly,° or worse, seemed to love it. "It's beautiful," said John J. Callahan, Jr., of Wildwood, New Jersey, a veteran who became antiwar after his return. "It's a black scar° in the ground—and Vietnam is a black scar on this country." Those who mourn the war as a noble cause, who feel betrayed by Richard Nixon's declaration of "peace with honor," tend to° despise the memorial. "It's black because we lost," said Will Howe of Port Hueneme, California, a three-times-wounded survivor of a bitter campaign in 1966. Howe, who brought his wife and two children three thousand miles across the country to see if the memorial was "as bad as everyone says its is," found himself agreeing that it was. "It could have been so different. I looked at the Seabee monument (in nearby Virginia)—it's nice, and it's simple," he said. "Everything else in this town is white."

a foolish mistake

mark of a wound

tend to: usually

From William Broyles Jr. in *Newsweek*

Like the war itself, the memorial is less than the dead deserved. It is a memorial that isn't a memorial for a war that wasn't, technically,° even a war. The war had no official beginning and no official end, only a first death and a last death. Its deepest meaning is in the fate of those who fought there. The veterans gave the war that meaning, and they and their families quickly, and spontaneously,° did the same for the memorial. Through countless acts of pure emotion, they completed a monument that seemed incomplete. It invited them, somehow, to make it their own. They propped° roses beside it, set photographs of dead sons and brothers on it, decorated with wreaths,° touched it constantly, and washed it with tears. But still, there was something missing, something special. The veterans, as they gathered last Wednesday and Thursday, couldn't quite put their fingers on° it, but they *knew.*

They would eventually solve that problem, but there was one thing about the monument they couldn't fix. The names that speak most directly about the war weren't on the memorial. To my knowledge there are no names of any sons or grandsons of the policymakers who plotted° the war or of the congressmen who voted the funds to keep it going. They weren't there. The war divided America, most of all by driving a wedge° between those who went and those who didn't.

officially

without planning

leaned
flower decoration

put their fingers on it: define

planned

driving a wedge: dividing

group of soldiers
country people

few

something in common
make use of/**by and large:** mostly

a game in which balls are rolled down an alley at a group of objects
stick used as walking aid

section

colored

The division was a matter of social class. In my Marine infantry platoon° were blacks from the South, ethnics from Chicago and Boston, hillbillies° from Appalachia, Mexican-Americans from Texas, and an Indian we called "Chief." Their average age was less than twenty; only a handful° had graduated from high school. They were working-class America. Not one of the boys who joined my platoon in the rice fields and jungles was the son of a doctor, lawyer, businessman, politician, or professor. In 1968, 6.8 million Americans were in college, about 500,000 Americans served in Vietnam, and there was virtually no overlap° between the two. The educated kids who knew how to manipulate° the system by and large° avoided the war; the less-privileged Americans fought and died there . . . .

And so from all over America, we went to Washington for our long-overdue homecoming. We brought parts of our old uniforms and a few of our medals. There were cowboys and union men and members of bowling° teams. There were men who walked with canes° and too many men in wheelchairs. Families came, some with new babies. A marine stopped before a panel,° found a name, and fell to his knees crying. Paul Rump of Thetford Center, Vermont, and a friend from Massachusetts brought the ashes of a fellow veteran who had killed himself. They scattered them in front of the panel that marked the year they were in Vietnam together. Then Rump and his friend embraced each other, and they wept.

I asked veteran Sid Smith, who is a sculptor in Florida, how he felt when he entered the monument.

"I cried," he replied.

"We all did," said Ed Unkel, a Marine from Cleveland. "We all did."

It was as if a common emotion held back in so many private corners was all at once coming out into the sunlight. I cried too, more than once. I cried for the men who had been there, for their families, for the country, for myself. I cried because I couldn't help it. It was beyond knowing. As I stood in front of the polished granite, I saw the names, but I also saw my own reflection. It fell across the names like a ghost. "Why me, Lord?" we asked ourselves in Vietnam. It was a question that came back as I stood there: "Why them?" It was a terrible sadness that brought the tears. But also, beneath it, there was a deep relief tinged° with guilt: my name isn't on the wall.

Around midnight on Thursday, a few Marines finally realized what the memorial was missing—a flag. And so, with the

In 1993 a second statue of three women helping a wounded soldier was placed nearby. This statue honors the 11,500 women who served in Vietnam—as nurses, intelligence analysts, air traffic controllers and in many other roles—as well as 265,000 other women who served in the military during the time of the war in Vietnam.

daring and skill that served them so well in Vietnam, they went on one last mission. Moving stealthily,° they borrowed a hotel's American flag and flagpole and went to the memorial. One of the Marines took the flag and stood motionless in the center of the memorial, where the two long courses of black granite meet to form a V. The others lit matches and shone flashlights on the flag. They sang "America," they swapped° stories, and they cried. "They didn't have to put up a flag for us," said Terry McConnell, a Marine from Cleveland who is unemployed. "We take care of our own. We always did; we always will."

secretly, quietly

exchanged

EXERCISES

I.   Find the Facts: True or False?

Write *T* if the statement is true and *F* if it's false.

_____   1.   The Vietnam Veterans Memorial was paid for by the U.S. government.

_____   2.   A national competition was held to select the design of the memorial.

_____   3.   The contestants in the competition were instructed to create a design "without political or military content."

_____   4.   A committee made up of Vietnam war veterans chose the winning entry in the contest.

_____   5.   The site of the memorial was paid for by the veterans.

_____   6.   Most war memorials are realistic statues depicting soldiers carrying weapons.

_____   7.   The Vietnam Veterans Memorial contains no flag or any reference to the war it commemorates.

_____   8.   The surface of the monument is smooth and highly polished.

_____   9.   The names of the soldiers who died are inscribed in alphabetical order.

_____   10.   In response to the outrage expressed by many veterans to the design of the memorial, it was decided that the monument would be replaced.

II.   A Closer Look

Most of this chapter is comprised of excerpts about the memorial from newspapers and magazines across the country. They reflect the range of reactions to the monument and also highlight many of the issues related to the controversies surrounding the war. Finding the answers to the following questions requires a careful reading of the text. Some of the answers cannot be found in any one excerpt but must be drawn from information throughout the chapter.

1.   The writer from the *New Republic* comments, "There are no inscriptions [on the monument] to tell you what to think." What effect does this omission have on the observer?

2.   The monument is comprised of a V-shaped slab of highly polished black stone inscribed with the names of those who died in the war. When observers read the names of the dead, their own faces are reflected on the surface. There are several references to this aspect of the design in the article. Discuss the various effects that this reflection has had on different observers.

3.   The Vietnam Veterans Memorial is situated between the Washington Monument and the Lincoln Memorial. You can see the reflections of these two historic landmarks on the surface of the Vietnam Veterans Memorial. Why do you think this is significant?

4. Many veterans were greatly angered by the design of the monument. What were some of their criticisms? What kind of monument had they expected?

5. Many have commented that the Vietnam Veterans Memorial is different from other war memorials because the war it commemorates differed greatly from previous wars. Explain this view.

6. Much of the controversy over the design of the monument has centered on the fact that it is the work of an "outsider." However, the writer from *Vogue* comments, "Perhaps only an outsider could have designed an environment which is so successful in answering the need for recognition by a group of people—the Vietnam vets—who are plagued by a sense of 'otherness' forced on them by a country that has spent ten years pretending not to see them." Why have Vietnam War veterans felt like "outsiders" in society?

7. In contrast to responses to other war memorials, where the visitor stands at a distance viewing a statue and an inscription, people have responded to the Vietnam Veterans Memorial in a unique way. Explain.

8. The following statement appears in the article by a Vietnam war veteran: "The war divided America, most of all by driving a wedge between those who went and those who didn't . . . . The division was a matter of class." Explain this statement.

9. Many veterans and the families of those who died in the war felt that the memorial was "less than the dead deserved." What did they do to "complete" the memorial?

III. Vocabulary in Context

Use context to choose the word or term that best fits the meaning of the italicized word in each sentence. Circle your choices.

1. The winning entry—a slab of black granite inscribed with the names of those who had died in Vietnam—immediately stirred up *controversy*. Some attacked the modern architectural style as inappropriate; others found it a particularly fitting choice for a memorial.

   a. enjoyment   b. difference of opinion   c. a large amount of money

2. The slabs have names on them. These were eager young men fighting in the jungles of Vietnam. Sometimes they thought they knew what they were doing; often they were *confused*.

   a. excited   b. uncertain   c. satisfied

3. Visitors were to walk down into the pit and come upon a black wall bearing the names of fifty-seven thousand dead men (and a few women)—with no explanations as to how, much less why, such a *dreadful* sacrifice took place.

   a. terrible   b. careful   c. hopeful

4. The veterans could have gotten any kind of sculpture they wanted—since they paid for the memorial with money they raised by themselves—had they not *come up with* the bright idea of turning the choice over to a jury of art experts.

    a. refused   b. laughed at   c. thought of

5. The veterans kept talking about a memorial "to honor and recognize those who served in Vietnam"; and, indeed, that phrase was written into the congressional order authorizing the veterans to *erect* the memorial on park land between the Lincoln Memorial and the Washington Monument.

    a. build   b. look for   c. use

6. It seems to me that Maya Lin's monument has been assaulted largely because it is *out of character.* Most people can scarcely imagine a monument without statues; to build one outside this convention seems a provocation.

    Out of character means

    a. boring   b. amusing   c. unusual

7. The *convention* referred to in Question 6 is that

    a. war memorials have statues.

    b. war memorials are not usually criticized.

    c. war memorials are large.

8. Perhaps only an "outsider" could have designed an environment which is so successful in answering the need for recognition by a group of people—the Vietnam vets—who are *plagued by* a sense of "otherness" forced on them by a country that has spent ten years pretending not to see them.

    a. proud of   b. believing in   c. suffering from

IV. Odd Man Out

Study the words in each group. Circle the one that is different.

1. judged   assaulted   attacked   criticized

2. revive   stir up   create   commemorate

3. reaction   conflict   controversy   battle

4. dreadful   impressive   shameful   insulting

5. powerful   awesome   moving   realistic

6. stigma   recognition   shame   dishonor

7. eager   dumbfounded   outraged   confused

8. inappropriate   fitting   deserved   proper

V.   Word Forms

Put the correct form of the word in each blank. Check the verb forms for correct tense, number, and voice (active or passive), and check the nouns for number (singular or plural).

1. dedication (n)   dedicate (v)   dedicated (adj)

    a. I admire him for his _____ to his work.

    b. The memorial _____ to all those who had died in the war.

    c. She's a very _____ teacher.

2. architect (n)   architecture (n)   architectural (adj)

    a. Frank Lloyd Wright was a famous American _____.

    b. Maya Lin is a graduate student in _____ at Yale University.

    c. Many considered the design of the new building an _____ achievement.

3. precision (n)   precise (adj)   precisely (adv)

    a. I did _____ what you asked me to.

    b. My mother is very _____ in her choice of words.

    c. The carpenter was well known for the _____ of his work.

4. funeral (n)   funereal (adj)

    a. The _____ will be held at Riverside Church tomorrow.

    b. The atmosphere at the office Christmas party was _____ because everyone knew that the company was going out of business.

5. authority (n)   authorization (n)   authorize (v)

    a. A congressional committee _____ an investigation of the problem.

    b. The criminal was captured by local _____, who then contacted the FBI.

    c. You are not permitted to enter this building without official _____.

6. eloquence (n)   eloquent (adj)   eloquently (adv)

    a. In her speech she _____ expressed the need for a different kind of political leadership.

    b. She spoke with _____ and passion.

    c. The senator delivered an _____ speech after losing the election.

7. hero (n)   heroism (n)   heroic (adj)

    a. The firefighter was praised for her _____ act.

    b. The soldier received a medal for his _____.

    c. When he returned home, he was greeted as a _____.

VI.   Sentence Completion

Complete each sentence, using one of the words listed below.

    in a dither   swapped   undeniable   slab   stark   propped   cite   dumbfounded

1. At the high-school reunion, everyone _____ stories about their teenage years.

2. She was _____ before the party, rushing around making sure all the arrangements had been made.

3. The _____ effect of the painting was created by the artist's use of black and white.

4. Let me _____ two examples to illustrate my point.

5. News of the invasion had a(n) _____ effect on the president's popularity.

6. The design of the Vietnam Veterans Memorial is a V-shaped _____ of highly polished granite.

7. When we entered the room, we found him sitting in bed, _____ up against the pillow, reading a comic book.

8. When we found out who had been appointed chairperson of the committee, we were _____; we hadn't realized that she was even being considered for the position.

COUNTERPARTS

1. In a small group, list the reasons given in the reading for and against the design of the Vietnam Veterans Memorial. Add your own ideas to the list. Based on these reasons, which group would you support? Argue your position in a debate with another group.

2. There are many memorials to war but few memorials to peace. The National Foundation for Peace in Washington, D.C. wants to build monuments to peace and peace heroes. What do you think a peace monument should look like? What individual, group, or event would you choose to represent peace? Where would you locate a peace monument? Design and then describe in writing your suggestion for a peace monument.

3. The photos on pages 158, 164, and 167 show different kinds of war memorials. Which monument do you think is a better memorial to war? Why?